JUDY BRISKY

THE JOY OF BEING MOM

DEVOTIONAL

Always an Adventure

GATEWAY® PRESS

TABLE OF CONTENTS

Section 3
THE LITTLE THINGS

Section 4
BEING MOM

Section 5
STAYING STRONG

Section 6
A LASTING LEGACY

Judy and her husband, Mike, have been close friends with my wife, Debbie, and me for more than 20 years. Over the years, we've watched Judy become one of the best mothers we've ever seen! We love how Judy writes this devotional to moms of all ages and stages of life. She shows how to have joy in every situation by giving an honest, front-row seat to her own personal journey as a mom—with all the victories and struggles. Rooted in God's Word, this devotional will inspire and encourage you to find the joy in being a mom as you embrace the adventure.

Robert and Debbie Morris
Senior Pastor of Gateway Church
Bestselling Author of *The Blessed Life, Beyond Blessed,*
and *Take the Day Off*

INTRODUCTION

For God is working in you, giving you the desire and the power to do what pleases him.

Philippians 2:13

Imagine you just woke up from a long, sleepless night. The baby seemed to want to nurse every hour. The toddler who usually sleeps through the night decided he'd rather stay up and play, and the older child had a stomachache. All on the same night.

The Scripture above tells us that the Father works in us to give us the desire and power to do what pleases Him. Guess what? It pleases God to help you be a mom to your little ones. It pleases Him to encourage you through His Word. It pleases Him to give you the energy and strength to do all that you do for your family. He loves you. He loves your children.

Whether your children are young or not so young, whether you're a morning person or a night person, whether you work in the house, out of the house, or both, you're a full-time working mom. Some days may be long and tough, but I promise you that despite your circumstances, you can know the joy of being Mom!

You may be wondering, *Really? Can I have that joy even when I'm tired, sleep-deprived, and overwhelmed?* Yes, you can! When nights like the one I mentioned (or something like it) occur, the Lord will give you what you need when you need it. He is always there for you. God doesn't tell us that things will always go smoothly, but He does promise to be with us through every sleepless night and tired morning.

When my sons were young, people would tell me that those early years fly by. Of course, I didn't believe them. Fly by? Not possible. But here I am with two grown, married sons who are now fathers! The years may not have "flown" by, but I must admit that they did go by pretty quickly.

Let me encourage you to enjoy the moment. Every moment. Prayerfully seek God's heart for your children and allow His love and wisdom to cover every hour of every day.

With love and joy,

Judy

PS: I recommend that you keep a journal as you read this devotional. Many of the suggested activities require some writing. As a mom, you probably have a long list of things to do, but I encourage you to take a few minutes every day to read one devotional with its accompanying prayer and activity. You may find that you actually like spending a little time jotting down your thoughts and ideas. Have fun reading!

PPS: You'll find a fun surprise at the end of this devotional. I'll give you a hint: you'll want to have your colored pencils available! Thank you to my daughter-in-love Danny Brisky for her beautiful artwork.

SECTION 1

THE CHRIST FOLLOWER

*But to all who believed him and accepted him, he gave the right
to become children of God.*

John 1:12

What is a Christ follower? What does a Christ-following mom need to help her care for her family? Our heavenly Father loves us so much and has made a way for all of us to be in right standing with Him through His Son, Jesus Christ. His strength and wisdom will help us in all we do. All we have to do is ask Him.

IS THIS ALL THERE IS?

But God is so rich in mercy, and he loved us so much, that even though we were dead because of our sins, he gave us life when he raised Christ from the dead. (It is only by God's grace that you have been saved!)

Ephesians 2:4–5

"Is this all there is?" That was the question my husband, Michael (he also goes by Mike), asked one rainy Sunday morning about a year into our marriage. "What is life really all about? We eat, work, and sleep, and then we do it all over again. Why? What's the point?" This was something we had discussed over the course of our relationship. We loved each other and were committed to our marriage, but what about life in general? Why were we here? What was the purpose?

As we talked, I suggested, "Why don't we read the Bible?" I found our Bible tucked away in our bedroom closet, and we opened it to a page that said something like, "If you've never read the Bible, start with the Book of John." I began to read:

In the beginning the Word already existed.
    The Word was with God,
    and the Word was God (John 1:1).

It was beautiful, amazing, and comforting. We made the decision to read the Bible every day.

Mike was a professional golfer at that time, and he was preparing to play some golf tournaments. To help with travel expenses, he would be rooming with another golfer on the road. We decided I would read the Bible to Mike over the phone because he was uncomfortable reading the hotel Bibles in front of his roommate. But it turned out that his roommate was a Christian who was planning to lead a Bible study on their golf tour.

A few months later, I visited my husband in Cary, North Carolina, and we attended the Bible study. We heard about salvation, which is also called being born again. I'd grown up believing that if I was a "good" person, then I'd go to heaven one day. Of course, "being good" was up to my interpretation. Mike and I learned that we have an enemy whose purpose is to keep us from following God. The enemy would have us believe that our mistakes—also called sins—are too great for us to be forgiven, but that is a lie. God is a faithful and kind Father, and because He loves us, He sent His only Son, Jesus Christ, to die for our sins so that we could be saved.

> God saved you by his grace when you believed. And you can't take credit for this; it is a gift from God. Salvation is not a reward for the good things we have done, so none of us can boast about it (Ephesians 2:8–9).

Grace is a free gift from God. When Jesus was crucified, He took our sins upon Himself and nailed them to the cross. The blood He shed covers every single sin we have ever committed or ever will commit.

Not only did Jesus die for our sins, but He also rose again on the third day. God's resurrection power raised Jesus from the dead, and this same power lives in us as His children when we accept Jesus as our Lord and Savior.

If you recognize your need for a Savior, please call out to the Lord right now and pray:

Dear God, I admit that I am a sinner. Today I surrender my life to You. I believe You sent Your Son, Jesus, to die on the cross for my sins, and He rose again on the third day. Jesus, I ask You to be my Lord and Savior. Thank You that I am completely forgiven and accepted into Your family. I choose to live for You from this day forward. In Jesus' name, Amen.

If you prayed this prayer, let me be the first one to say, "Welcome to the family of God!" He will never leave you. The blood of Jesus covers all your sins—past, present, and future. Now, there may be consequences for choices made in the past. There may be relationships that need mending or situations that need to be addressed. But God will be with you every step of the way. He will give you wisdom and strength as you move forward and live for Him.

LET'S PRAY

Thank You, Father, for Your love and for the gift of salvation. Thank You that the blood of Jesus paid the price for all my sins! I'm so grateful for Your Word and for the assurance that You are always there for me. Help me be the mom you've called me to be and give me wisdom in all I do. In Jesus' name, Amen.

ACTIVITY

Write a love letter to the Lord, thanking Him for His gift of salvation. You may want to write down your salvation story (how you came to know Jesus as your Lord and Savior). It will serve as a beautiful reminder to you that the Lord loves you and is there to help you in all you do.

DAY 2

GOD'S LOVE LETTER

For the word of the Lord holds true,
and we can trust everything he does.

Psalm 33:4

I keep several boxes in our bedroom closet that contain lots of letters and cards Mike and I mailed to each other during our dating years. He lived in a nearby town, but we couldn't see each other regularly, so writing was our main way of communication (other than the occasional phone call). You may wonder, *Couldn't you just talk on the phone every day?* Actually, no, we couldn't. Mike's world was full of school and work and golf and family commitments, so writing became our primary form of staying connected. To this day, I *love* getting cards and notes from my guy. Once in a while, I like to pull out a box of old letters and read them. My husband was (and continues to be) quite the romantic.

Mike's letters remind me of our early days when we fell in love and knew we would do life together. As Christians, we too have a love letter—the greatest love letter of all time. The Bible tells us all about God's love for us, beginning with Genesis (the story of how our world came to be) and ending with Revelation (the story of how we will live for eternity with God in heaven). Of course, there's so much more to learn between these two writings.

The Bible is the most important book you will ever read. Why is it considered God's love letter? Because from beginning to end, the consistent thread is that God loves us and desires to have relationship with us through His Son, Jesus Christ.

When we read the Bible, we should begin by asking God to guide us and help us understand what we read in His Word. It may feel like there's too much to learn, but He will help you! God's Word will bring encouragement when you need it and direction when you're unsure of what to do. As you spend time reading each day, you will grow in your love for the Lord and in your life as a follower of Jesus Christ. God's Word is our constant reassurance of His love and care for us in every moment of every day.

LET'S PRAY

Father, I am so grateful that we have the Bible to help us learn more about You and Your love for us. I'm thankful that I can find truth and life in this beautiful letter written by You. Please help me know You more each time I read it. May my heart, mind, and soul always hunger for Your living Word. In Jesus' name, Amen.

ACTIVITY

It takes discipline to develop any new habit in life. To help you spend time each day in the Word, I recommend taking your calendar (whether physical or digital) and writing "Bible" on each day for the next month. It will serve as a reminder to take some time to read every day. Before you know it, you'll be reaching for your Bible without even seeing it on your calendar! Don't wait for the "perfect" time. Start today!

THANK YOU NOTES

Enter his gates with thanksgiving;
go into his courts with praise.
Give thanks to him and praise his name.

Psalm 100:4

I've never been very good at writing thank you notes. I always have great intentions, and sometimes I actually write them, but then I forget to mail them. This isn't something I would normally share, but in light of writing about being thankful, I thought I'd come clean.

One thing I have done for quite a few years now is thank the Lord every night for 10 things. I call it my daily "Top 10" thank you list. It's something I start my prayers with every night. Yes, if I'm really tired, I may fall asleep before saying every thank you, but it's something that has become an important part of my life. The Scripture above is a reminder that our hearts of praise and gratitude give us entrance into the presence of our God. That alone is reason enough to nurture a life of thanksgiving!

Most nights I'm quick to list off more than 10 things, but on the rare occasion that I get stuck, I mentally replay my day. I think about what I've done, whom I've spoken to, where I've gone, and what brought a smile to my face during the day.

Perhaps I heard from a friend through a text or phone call. Maybe I found my favorite blouse tucked in the back of my closet. I have found that developing a thankful heart begins with being grateful for those things that we may consider normal or mundane. For example, having my dad empty the dishwasher is always a welcome treat! The small occurrences throughout daily life are what make up our world. When we can appreciate them, they become the things we are grateful for every day. These simple patterns and rhythms of daily living become treasures when we value them.

Being Mom will bring different seasons, yet they will all have their routines and familiarity. It's these seemingly insignificant occurrences that remind us of all we have to be thankful for each and every day.

Oh, and those sometimes written but rarely sent thank you notes? I'm going to start making them part of my daily to dos. Now, that's something to put on my "Top 10" list!

LET'S PRAY

Father, I love You, and I am truly thankful for all You have done and continue to do in my life. May I always remember those things, both small and large, that make up my world! Please give me a heart of thanksgiving for all the joys of being Your daughter. In Jesus' name, Amen.

ACTIVITY

Set aside a journal for each of your children and one for yourself. Each day for a week, have your children write down 10 things they are thankful for before bedtime. If they are too little to write, write it down for them. You do the same, and at the end of the week read over your lists together. Talk about them and do it again the following week. You may begin a family tradition of "Thankful Journaling"! This family activity will be a sweet reminder that there is always so much to be thankful for each day.

DAY 4

TIMES OF QUIET

Truly my soul finds rest in God;
my salvation comes from him.

Psalm 62:1 (NIV)

As a little boy, our son Jacob was always an early riser. His younger brother Joel, on the other hand, liked his sleep. One day, Joel complained that Jacob was waking him up in the morning. After a little investigating on my part, it turned out that while Joel slept, Jacob would come up to his bed and whisper ever so softly, "Joel, Joel, are you awake? Are you awake, Joel?" He would do this until Joel woke up. Then Jacob would say, "Joel's awake now!"

Honestly, I found it very sweet that Jacob couldn't wait for his little brother to wake up so they could play together. He missed him and wanted time with him.

I think that's how our heavenly Father feels about us. He wants to spend time with us, whether it's in the morning or bedtime or somewhere in between. If you've felt those promptings in your heart to spend time with the Lord through prayer and reading His Word, perhaps He's whispering ever so lightly in your ear and in your heart. God, who created the heavens and the earth, desires to spend time with you. Why? Because He loves you, and He wants to encourage you.

When Mike and I became parents, we recognized the importance of spending time with the Father on a daily basis. Over the years, our times of prayer and reading changed depending on the season our children were in at the moment. For example, when there are babies to feed and diapers to be changed around the clock, your "quiet time" with the Lord may take place in the middle of the night. When little ones are running around, you may pray and read during naps or bathroom breaks. As the littles get a bit older, you'll teach them about having quiet times, and you can have them together. Reading the Bible together is a fun way to discuss what you're reading and hear what's on your children's minds as well.

Before you know it, your children will be having quiet times of their own, and they'll be sharing with you what God has put on their hearts!

LET'S PRAY

Father, may I never be too busy to spend time with You every day. When my days are full and rest seems far away, remind me that my time with You is what truly refreshes my heart. Your Word brings life, and in Your presence is fullness of joy! In Jesus' name, Amen.

ACTIVITY

Try placing your Bible where you will see it every day. A few places might be near the coffee maker, on the bathroom counter, or on the table where you sit to eat meals. Placing it in areas that you frequent daily will help you remember to spend time in the Word. Before you know it, you'll find that you are looking forward to this daily time with your heavenly Father.

JUST ONE THING

Your word is a lamp to guide my feet
and a light for my path.

Psalm 119:105

Is it just me or do you have those days where you wake up and your plan to have that quiet time with the Lord doesn't go as scheduled? You get your Bible, your pen, and your cup of coffee, and then it starts. The thoughts begin rushing in:

- *Let me check my emails just in case there's something I need to take care of right away.*
- *I wonder what's new on social media.*
- *I really need to start that load of laundry. Oops! I left the previous load in the washer overnight.*
- *I'll start reading as soon as I make that appointment.*
- *Just one phone call, and then I'll sit down and get started.*

Before you know it, it's bedtime, and you're in the midst of one or more of the following:

- The baby's diaper needs to be changed.
- The toddler needs to be tucked into bed.
- The child needs a new glove for baseball practice by tomorrow.
- The teenager needs to talk—right now!

Finally in bed, you're exhausted and can't see clearly enough to read. You tell yourself, *It'll be different tomorrow. I'll definitely start my day by getting in the Word!* The next morning the alarm goes off, but you don't hear it, and the cycle begins again.

Even when your children are adults with families of their own, it's easy to get sidetracked with "just one more thing." Before you know it, one more thing turns into many more things, and your time with the Lord is lost in your whirlwind of a day. What to do?

First of all, let me share my heart. The idea to write this particular devotion came to mind one morning when I found myself hours into my day and not yet having sat still to read my Bible. I'd begun to do "just one more thing," and hours later I was still doing one more thing. The truth is, it happens to all of us. The important thing is to keep it from being a regular occurrence. "Just how do we do that?" you may ask. We have to make getting in the Word a priority. Whether you decide to read early in the morning before anyone else is awake or at night when all is quiet, it must be an appointment that you choose to keep every day. If you're already reading regularly, you know the difference it makes in your life.

When you have babies and/or littles at your feet, it can be hard to find even a few minutes in an already full day. Here's an idea: memorize some Scriptures that speak to your heart. You can memorize one of the Psalms or any other verses or chapters. Before my first baby was born, I memorized Psalm 23 because I knew there would be days when I may not open my Bible.

Memorizing Scripture is good whether we have littles or not. Having the Word of God planted in our hearts and minds is a sure way to keep us grounded in our Christian walk. God's Word gives us clarity, direction, peace, wisdom, and so much more. Today is a good day to start!

LET'S PRAY

Father, I know that Your Word brings life, peace, wisdom, and so many other wonderful things. When my days are full, help me focus on what's at hand and make time to spend with You. You are my heart's desire, and Your Word is what I need to grow in You! In Jesus' name, Amen.

ACTIVITY

What Scriptures can you start memorizing? Psalms and Proverbs are good places to start. Perhaps there's a chapter or even a book of the Bible that you can begin to put to memory today. There's no time limit on memorizing God's Word. Just start today—one word, sentence, or paragraph at a time.

PRAYERFUL CONNECTIONS

I call on you, my God, for you will answer me;
turn your ear to me and hear my prayer.

Psalm 17:6 (NIV)

A s a little girl, I talked to God all the time. For me, that was what praying was all about. I would sometimes feel scared or lonely at night, so I would ask Jesus to hold me. I would imagine Him being right next to me, holding me in His arms. I'm telling you; I could feel His arms around me. The Lord was always very real to me.

During my grade school years, I attended a denominational church where prayers were memorized and recited regularly, but even then I really tried to think about what I was saying. When I came to know Jesus as my Lord and Savior over 30 years ago, praying came naturally to me. When I spoke to God, I really expected to hear back from Him. Perhaps not audibly but certainly through His Word, through others, or through the Holy Spirit.

When it comes to praying, there is no right or wrong way to do it. Each of us will do things differently because we are created differently. You may like to journal for hours at a time. Sometimes I like to listen to worship for a while before praying. You may like to have a cup of tea with Jesus. I have coffee. The important thing is that we spend time with the Lord in prayer. He loves us and really wants to talk to us too!

When we pray, several things happen in our lives. First, we build our relationship with God by sharing our thoughts, needs, concerns, and gratitude. Second, praying is an acknowledgement that we need the Lord because we are unable to live life by our own strength. We need Him! Third, our prayers are an act of worship. Our words of love, adoration, and thanksgiving are a daily affirmation that God is sovereign, all-knowing, and all-powerful.

I know moms with young children may find it difficult to set aside a designated time to pray. However, I'm sure you've already come to realize that when you make it a priority to spend time with God every day, it makes a huge difference in your life. You'll find that you have more peace, strength, wisdom, and energy. Remember, we aren't limited to praying only when we need something or have a problem.

> Are any of you suffering hardships? You should pray. Are any of you happy? You should sing praises (James 5:13).

Whether you seek the Lord for a need or praise Him for an answered prayer, make time to talk to Him every day. He's always ready to listen.

LET'S PRAY

Father, I am so thankful that You are always there for me and ready to listen as I share my heart's concerns as well as my joys. Thank You for being such a good and kind Father. I am overwhelmed by Your love! In Jesus' name, Amen.

ACTIVITY

Try journaling your prayer requests for this week or month. When a prayer is answered, write it down next to the request you made. This is a tangible way to see how the Lord is working in your life. You may find that you like doing this every day!

HERE & THERE PRAYERS

Devote yourselves to prayer with an alert mind and a thankful heart.

Colossians 4:2

When my sons were young, they knew that praying was something I did throughout the day. It wasn't something that we relegated only to meals and before bedtime. I wanted them to know that prayer was a way of life. It was something we could do all day long, because praying is simply talking to God. Yes, we may have requests, but prayer is more than that. It's also sharing our heart with the Lord, telling Him our thoughts and feelings and giving Him our gratitude. These are things that happen throughout the day, and when we make talking to God a regular part of our schedule, our hearts become more in tune with the Lord and what He wants for us.

For example, if we were driving and heard a siren, I'd pray for the people who might be involved in a car accident. If I knew of someone who was sick, we would pray for their healing. There were even a few times when a driver did something that was ... well, not very wise. The boys knew I might not be happy about it, but I would say, "Let's pray for that driver. They need some prayer right now!"

Mike and I wanted our sons to know that prayer was something we did every day, all day long. While it's important to pray for our families, world events, and every other subject or situation, the Scripture at the beginning of this devotion also directs us to pray with a thankful heart. It is our thankfulness that gives us entry into the presence of God.

Let us come to him with thanksgiving.
Let us sing psalms of praise to him (Psalm 95:2).

How beautiful for our children to grasp that having a thankful heart welcomes us into God's presence! Prayer and thanksgiving go hand in hand. When we make praying a part of our everyday lives, we teach our children that talking to God is something they can do all the time, because He is always there to listen.

LET'S PRAY

Father, I am so grateful that You are always available to hear me. You're never too busy to hear the cries of my heart, no matter how many times I come to You each day. You care about every concern, need, and hurt that weighs me down, and You rejoice with every victory! Thank You for always being there for my family and me. You are such a good Father. In Jesus' name, Amen.

ACTIVITY

Ask your children each day if there's anything they'd like to pray about. This will help them develop a strong prayer life and know that there is nothing too big or too small for our God. It also serves to remind us that we, too, are His children, and He's always ready to listen to our hearts.

DO YOU HEAR ME?

*Such things were written in the Scriptures long ago to teach us.
And the Scriptures give us hope and encouragement as we wait
patiently for God's promises to be fulfilled.*

Romans 15:4

We had recently miscarried our first baby. Mike was back on the road playing golf, and I was home recovering (physically and mentally) from our loss. One night as I unsuccessfully tried to fall asleep, I asked the Lord to give me a verse to calm my mind and heart so that I could sleep. As I was praying, I heard in my spirit, "Psalm 4, verse 8." I turned on the lamp on my nightstand, reached for my Bible, and went to the book of Psalms. Had I heard Him right? Had God really spoken to my heart and led me to a specific verse? I believed He had, and I was searching for this answer to my prayer. I got to Psalm 4 and looked for verse 8. I saw verse 5, then 6 and wondered, *Is there a verse 8?* Yes! There it was.

In peace I will lie down and sleep,
    for you alone, Lord,
        make me dwell in safety (Psalm 4:8 NIV).

To say I was overwhelmed by God's love and kindness would be an understatement. I had cried out to Him in my sadness, and He had spoken. His Word brought me peace, and most of all, it brought me to the realization that He hears me, knows me, sees me, and loves me.

What I realized more than anything else is that God's Word will always bring us a clearer picture of who He is and who we are in Him.

- We are fearfully and wonderfully made (see Psalm 139:14).
- We can be confident that He works all things for our good (see Romans 8:28).
- We can trust Him (see Proverbs 3:5–6).
- We are saved by grace through faith (Ephesians 2:8–10).
- We are loved (see John 3:16).

That night God spoke to me. It wasn't an audible voice, but His heart spoke to mine. It brought rest, peace, and love. Since that night, my faithful Father has continued to speak to me over the course of my life. Sometimes He may speak a word of encouragement through others, but mostly He speaks to me through His Word and His promptings in my heart. How do I know it's Him? Because nothing I hear should ever contradict His Word. His Word is true today and always!

Make space in your heart to hear Him today. Make space in your world to allow His Living Word to bring you peace, wisdom, and guidance. Most importantly, invite Jesus Christ, God in the flesh, to reign over your life.

LET'S PRAY

Father, help me make space in my heart, my mind, and my entire being so that the Lord Jesus can have all the room to live in me. In my weakest moments, hold my heart. In my joy-filled days, hold my hand. And in all the in-between days, hold me close. I love You. In Jesus' name, Amen.

ACTIVITY

Has the Lord "given" you a special Scripture? If so, write it down and place it where you can see it every day. It will encourage you and remind you that you hear Him and He hears you too.

PRAYING WHEN IT'S HARD

Answer me when I call to you,
my righteous God.
Give me relief from my distress;
have mercy on me and hear my prayer.

Psalm 4:1 (NIV)

Praying builds our trust in God regardless of whether our requests are answered in the way we would like for them to be. Our trust comes from moments spent in His presence. Pouring out our heart's needs, desires, hurts, and joys gives us an opportunity to connect with our heavenly Father. These times of prayer allow us to empty our souls to Him, but what's even better is that when we make time to pray and listen, the miraculous can happen.

When Joel, our second son, was four years old, he started having leg pain. It wasn't a regular occurrence, and we thought it was "growing pains." When he started having the pain more regularly, we scheduled an appointment to see the doctor. A check-up led to x-rays, which showed a spot on Joel's hip. An MRI was scheduled, and although we were concerned, Mike and I prayed that God would heal anything that might be wrong. When the MRI results came in, our doctor called with the good news. All was well. He went on to say that he had thought Joel had cancer, and he believed we had received a miracle. We agreed. Mike and I were thrilled and grateful that the Lord had healed our son.

Fast forward to our fifth child. We were excited to learn that we were having another baby. Our sons went with us on the day we were scheduled to find out if we were having a boy or girl. The doctor quickly said it was a girl, but our joy was short-lived. After having the nurse take our sons out of the room, he told us that he could see that our baby had numerous health issues. He talked. I cried. It was shocking to hear that our girl would likely die before she entered the world. We had faced possible bad news before with our son, so we were determined to fight on our knees for our Danielle. (That's what we named her—Michaela Danielle. We called her Dani.)

I didn't pray any differently for Dani than I had for Joel years before. Both times I was on my knees crying out to God. Many others interceded on our behalf, too. However, Dani's story ended differently. Our baby girl passed away after living with us for just over two months. Although the outcome was not what we'd hoped for, she had surpassed what the doctors had told us. She was a miracle, and we were grateful to have had her with us even for a short time.

Losing our Dani was probably the most difficult and painful time in my life, but it was also the most precious time in my relationship with God. I learned to trust Him completely. Trusting Him doesn't mean I understood what happened. It simply means that I chose to trust Him no matter the outcome. For me, trusting God means giving up my desire to understand most things. One thing I do understand, though, is that God loves me, and He cares for me and my family. That's enough. Actually, it's more than enough.

LET'S PRAY

Father, thank You that having Your love is more than enough. In the most trying circumstances, knowing that You love me has been the sweetest thing in my life. When my prayers are answered the way I would like, I have learned to trust You. When my prayers are not answered the way I would like, I have also learned to trust You. My entire life is about trusting You, and my prayer life has served to help me trust You more, regardless of any outcome. In Jesus' name, Amen.

ACTIVITY

Make a list of the things your family is praying for this season. This will allow your husband and children to join in prayer with you and with each other. Rejoice together when a prayer is answered. Thank the Lord for His strength when a prayer isn't answered in the way you would have preferred. In every outcome, praise the Lord for always listening to, always caring for, and always loving you.

PRAYING GOD'S WORD

Devote yourselves to prayer with an alert mind and a thankful heart.

Colossians 4:2

When we are devoted to prayer it, means that we persevere in our devotion. Now add to that an alert mind, and you have someone who is devoted to prayer and taking this responsibility to heart by not allowing their mind to wander to other things or concerns. This is a prayer warrior who is persevering in calling out to God and staying in tune with the Lord, all while maintaining a posture of thanksgiving. Thankfulness brings us into God's presence, and that's where we open our hearts and minds and give Him praise (see Psalm 100:4).

One thing I love to do is read the Word and insert my husband's name, my family and friends' names, and my name into the Scriptures. When I do this, I am declaring the mighty and living Word of God over the lives and circumstances I'm bringing before the Father.

In those moments when you may not know what to pray, praying God's Word is always a great idea. His Word brings life, healing, and wisdom, and when our words are few, His are always plentiful and perfect. When our baby girl was still with us, there were numerous times when I didn't know what to pray. Yes, I prayed for healing, but reading God's Word made the circumstances more bearable. I can still picture in my mind when Mike held Dani in one arm, held his Bible in the other, and read God's Word over her. This moment is engrained in my mind and still brings me so much comfort. That is one of the many benefits of reading God's Word over your life and the lives of your loved ones. The Bible brings us comfort, healing, encouragement, strength ... the list goes on and on. Most importantly, the Word reminds us of His never-ending love.

We love each other because he loved us first (1 John 4:19).

One way we show our love for others is by praying for them. What better prayer than speaking God's Word over those we love!

LET'S PRAY

Father, how wonderful it is that when we can't find the words to say, we can go to our Bible and speak Your words over those we love. Thank You for giving us Your life-giving Word that we can pray over our families and friends every day in every situation. In Jesus' name, Amen.

ACTIVITY

Have each of your family members, including yourself, select a favorite Scripture. Share it and pray it over each other every day for a week. At the end of the week, each person can choose to keep the verse or select a new verse for the following week. Write your verse in your prayer journal as a remembrance.

SECTION 2

WE ARE FAMILY

But the love of the Lord remains forever
with those who fear him.
His salvation extends to the children's children
of those who are faithful to his covenant,
of those who obey his commandments!

Psalm 103:17–18

W hile every family is unique, we as Christians have similarities in the way we live our lives. These include our hearts' desire to follow God and His Word and choosing to live each day for Him in all we do as women, wives, and moms. When we live for God, our daily lives will reflect His heart in our marriages, families, and homes.

DAY 11

ALL MY CHILDREN

How precious are your thoughts about me, O God.
They cannot be numbered!

Psalm 139:17

I
f you ever wonder how much God loves you or how often He thinks of you, all you need to do is remember this verse. His thoughts for you and your children are precious and countless. What a gift!

After I accepted Jesus as the Lord of my life, one of the first things that changed was my desire to be a mom. When Mike and I got married, he knew I didn't want to have children. I loved children, but I didn't want any of my own because I was scared. What if my children got made fun of, bullied, or hurt in some way? What if I couldn't protect them? I honestly didn't think my heart could handle that. Once I got saved, though, I had a different outlook. God changed my heart and exchanged fear with faith.

We have five children, three of whom are in heaven. We miscarried our first baby, and months later we got pregnant with our first son Jacob. Little brother Joel was born just over two years later, followed by Jared, whom we lost when I was just under 20 weeks pregnant. Our fifth child was Danielle (Dani). Dani was born with a rare chromosomal abnormality and died two months and six days after she was born. Each of my children is a gift, and I am thankful for every one of them.

Before Dani was born, a friend mentioned to me that she had asked the Lord to give her a word for each of her children while she was pregnant. I loved the idea and decided I would do that as well. The verse above is a reminder of how God sees us and how lovingly He thinks of us. When we ask Him, I believe He will help us see our children with His eyes, and He will give us a word of encouragement for each one.

For our first baby, whom we lost early in our pregnancy, the word I received was "I (God) am in control." While I make daily decisions, God is ultimately in control of everything. I can choose to trust Him, or I can try to manipulate my circumstances. The first choice brings peace; the second brings stress. For Jacob, the Lord gave me the word "joy," which describes my son perfectly. He sees the bright side of every situation and the good in every person. For Joel, God gave me the word "love"; Joel loves deeply and has a smile that makes others feel welcome, seen, and cared for. The Lord gave me the word "strength" for Jared. God's strength carried me through the loss of our son. For Dani, the Lord gave me the word "miracle," Medically speaking, she was not supposed to live, but God made a way for her to come into the world. Her short life impacted many and continues to do so.

I am also blessed with two beautiful daughters-in-love. Having these incredible women in my life is one of my greatest joys. The word God put on my heart for my girls is "treasure." These lovely ladies are of great worth and value to me and our family.

The words God has given me for each of my children are gifts straight from the Father's heart. They are reminders that all my children are unique and loved and seen by God and me.

LET'S PRAY

Father, thank You for my children! Every single one is a gift and a blessing. We treasure those who are still with us on earth, and for those who are already in heaven, we rejoice that they are in Your presence. Please help us find joy in every season of being Mom. In Jesus' name, Amen.

ACTIVITY

If you have a God-given word for each of your children, write them down and have them framed. They will serve as lasting reminders of the gifts your children are to your family. If you've never asked the Lord for a word for your littles, now is the time! Pray and seek the Father's heart for each one. What a joy it will be when you share these words with your children.

FOUNDATION MATTERS

When the storms of life come, the wicked are whirled away,
but the godly have a lasting foundation.

Proverbs 10:25

As I've been working on this devotional, my younger son and his wife have been house hunting. While the number of bedrooms and bathrooms is important, as well as the aesthetics, the most important thing they look for is that the house has a good foundation. When there are signs of cracks in the walls, ceilings, or floors, there could be foundation problems. However, not all cracks are created equal. Some situations may just need an easy repair while others will require substantial work. Over time, if a foundation is not secure, the damage from erosion or storms can become severe, and the cost to repair such damage can also be greater. The bottom line is this: how a house will stand the test of time depends on how solid the foundation is.

The same is true for our lives. We need to be planted in the strong and spiritual foundation that is found in Jesus Christ. Being a Christian doesn't mean we won't go through difficult situations or endure painful events. We still live in a broken world. Our relationship with God, however, gives us hope and strength in every circumstance and battle that we may face.

When we invite God into our lives, He lays the foundation and begins to remodel our hearts and minds.

Making changes to our homes requires moving things around or removing them completely. There are often heavy items that require help to move, whether to a different spot or out of the house entirely. In the same way, God will remove things that would keep us from living the life He has planned for us. There may be habits that need to be broken, relationships that need mending, or unhealthy choices that need to be addressed.

The process of remodeling our lives may not be easy or comfortable, but I can promise you that it will be worth it! God loves you so much, and He wants you to live a healthy, joy-filled life. His plans for you are good, and He can be trusted with every detail.

LET'S PRAY

Father, I invite You to move whatever needs to be moved from my heart, my mind, and my life. I want to have a firm foundation that is completely made and dependent on You! Thank You for giving me all I need to stand firmly in You and in Your Word. In Jesus' name, Amen.

ACTIVITY

Draw a picture of the outside of your home, including the trees and any foliage. Ask the Lord to give you a Scripture for your home that you can write on the bottom of your drawing. Frame and hang it where you can see it every day as a reminder that your life, family, and home are built on God's firm foundation. If your children are old enough to draw, have each of them draw a picture that they can hang in their rooms.

HOME BUILDERS

For every house has a builder, but the one who built everything is God.

Hebrews 3:4

W e have our houses built by a team of people who know what they are doing. These people measure, cut, nail, and do a flurry of other things that end up building a house where people live, grow, and do life. Ultimately, God is the Master Builder of all things, both in the natural and spiritual realms.

Mike and I had a nice place to live when we were first married. Although it was a small apartment, we fixed it up nicely and enjoyed it for a season. A few years later, we were able to purchase a house. Was it bigger? Yes. Was it nicer? Yes. What made it really special? The presence of the Lord dwelled there. God's presence had nothing to do with the size or décor or any "thing." He filled our house because we had invited Him into our hearts, our lives, and our home. Actually, I should say we welcomed Him into "His" home. When we became Christians a year into our marriage, we realized that everything we have belongs to Him. We are merely stewards of every blessing, and that includes our home.

When we look at a house as a symbol of God and His family, it takes on a different meaning. It goes from being a house to being a home. Now, it is more than lumber and nails; it is something that will provide shelter, community, love, and joy. Home represents commitment, stability, and a sense of permanence. When we invite Him in, God turns our houses into homes where His presence is welcome and known by all who enter. And when I say houses/homes, I mean any place you live. It could be an apartment, a room in someone else's home, or a rental house. The size, space, or type of dwelling doesn't matter. Home is not defined by size but by love—the love God brings and the love we extend to others.

When the Jesus becomes your Lord and Savior, He takes the reigns as Master Builder. This is not only for the home you live in but for your life as well. Allow Jesus to have full access to every part of your home and life and see what remodeling He'll do to make your life a greater reflection of His love to those around you. While decorating is fun and makes our homes more beautiful, when Christ dwells there, you'll see the supernatural beauty of love, compassion, forgiveness, and all those godly qualities that make a house a home and a group of people a family.

LET'S PRAY

Father, thank You for my home and for my family, as well as all those You have brought into my life. I am thankful to be able to share Your love and hospitality with others. Help me to extend You heart to those You put on my path. In Jesus' name, Amen.

ACTIVITY

As a family, prayerfully seek God's heart for your home. How would He have you describe it? Fun? Happy? Loving? Creative?

Peaceful? The list goes on and on. One word may stand out to you, or it may be a few words or a phrase. It will be a fun family activity to do together. Once you have your word(s), make a sign and have it framed for your home.

DAY 14

KEEPING HOUSE

She also rises while it is yet night,
And provides food for her household,
And a portion for her maidservants.

Proverbs 31:15 (NKJV)

She's up before dawn, preparing breakfast
for her family and organizing her day.

Proverbs 31:15 (MSG)

'm one of those people who loves organizing and reading about organizing. Now, that doesn't mean I'm super organized, but it does mean I'm always trying. If you're like me, having things fairly in order makes the world a happier place. There's nothing like looking for something and actually finding it in the first place you look! Realistically, though, when there are littles (and not so littles), tasks such as eating and wearing clean clothes take priority.

Before our sons got married, they were a huge help in keeping our home running smoothly. They helped clean, and as they got older, they did their own laundry. I wanted them to be able to help their future wives one day. They were such a big part of getting things ready for parties and gatherings that when they married, it took me awhile to be able to get things organized on my own!

I once spoke to a mom who felt guilty about asking her children to help with chores around the house. My encouragement to her was that it's a disservice to our children *not* to teach and allow them to help care for our homes. Including our children in keeping our homes in order teaches them to work together and to be helpful around the house.

I have found that when we make it a family activity to help with things around the house, we're telling our children that we are a team that helps each other and works together to have a nice home. I remember one day when the boys were young, Joel asked, "Who's coming over?" He thought that because we were cleaning, we must be having company over that evening. That served as a reminder to both of us. I told him we weren't having guests over; instead, we were cleaning for ourselves so that our home would be nice and comfortable for our family. I reminded myself that I needed to be more aware of the message I was sending that appeared to imply we cleaned only when guests were coming.

You'll find an abundance of "keeping house" ideas online and from organized friends and family. However, the best ideas will come from asking the Lord what He wants you to focus on as you care for your home. While keeping the house clean is a good idea, stressing about it doesn't help. As in everything else, God knows what needs to be done, and He will direct your steps.

Our son Jacob and his family recently spent two wonderful weeks with us. Our days were filled with playing with grandbabies, eating yummy food, going out for fun adventures, and visiting with family and friends. There was no time for regular cleaning and keeping things organized. Family and friends will *always* trump cleaning!

Consequently, as I write this, our master bedroom and closet are pretty filled (overflowing, actually) with all kinds of things. And you know what? I'm okay with that. There will be days and sometimes seasons when a little messy is the norm. In those times, do what you can when you can. On this side of being Mom, I have found that memory-making far outweighs cleaning.

LET'S PRAY

Father, I'm grateful for my family and for our home. Help me balance keeping a clean and orderly home with having a place of warmth and hospitality. Give me wisdom as I seek to make it a space where everyone feels welcome and loved. May my words bring life, and may my actions speak love. Most importantly, may Your presence dwell in our midst. In Jesus' name, Amen.

ACTIVITY

Prayerfully determine what you and yours can do to make your home a refuge of rest and refreshment. If you're married, ask your spouse for his input. If you have older children, ask what a restful home looks like to them. These family discussions will help you as you seek the Father's heart for your home.

WASHING FEET

So he got up from the table, took off His robe, wrapped a towel around His waist, and poured water into a basin. Then he began to wash the disciples' feet, drying them with the towel he had around him.

John 13:4–5

The twelve disciples were sitting around the table for what would be their last meal together before the Lord's crucifixion. Jesus stood, removed His outer garment, and proceeded to wash their feet. In those days, the lowest form of servitude was foot washing. When men would arrive at someone's home, their feet would likely be dusty and dirty, and servants would see to washing them. Our Savior took on the role of a servant when He washed the feet of His disciples. The Son of God, who would soon take on the sins of the world in order to offer all humanity eternal life, was washing dirty feet with the hands that would soon be nailed to a cross.

For years, I wondered, *Why did Jesus remove His outer garment before washing the disciples' feet?* Practically speaking, it's possible that He didn't want His covering to get wet as He washed the men's feet, but surely there was more to it than that. One day, as I was doing some studying, I learned that in Jesus' time, one's outer garments represented his status in society. When Jesus removed His outer garment and laid it aside, I believe He was laying aside who He was—the Son of God and soon-to-be Savior of all mankind. Jesus chose to be a servant. More than that, His actions represented His laying His life down for His children. The Lord was showing us, as well as everyone who would read His Word, that when we serve others, we are laying aside our personal wants and desires. That's what we do being Mom, isn't it? Many times we lay down our own wants and desires for the immediate needs of our children. We make sacrifices to love, serve, and care for them. I believe that when we do this, we are most in alignment with Christ's heart for us.

> But among you it will be different. Whoever wants to be a leader among you must be your servant, and whoever wants to be first among you must become your slave. For even the Son of Man came not to be served but to serve others and to give his life as a ransom for many (Matthew 20:26–28).

As a little boy, Joel loved being outside and playing in the dirt. I reminded him regularly to wipe his feet before coming into the house. One day, after a recent rain, I heard the door open. There stood my son, with both bare feet covered in mud. I thought I was going to be upset, but his cute, three-year-old face just looked at me, seemingly wondering what I was going to do. I walked over to him, picked him up, and held him in my arms without saying a word. We went to the bathroom, and I sat him on the counter. I turned on the water, and we both waited silently for the water to warm up. After filling the sink, I put his muddy little feet in the warm water and gently washed them off with soap. When I was done, I dried his feet, hugged him, and gave him lots of kisses. He gave me the biggest smile. Then I said he could go back outside to play.

After all these years, that moment still stands out in my mind. It serves as a reminder of how we're called to serve those we love. Life gets messy, and sometimes, instead of getting upset about it, we can show love and patience. Interestingly, Joel doesn't recall any of this. At first, I was a little sad that he didn't remember what was such a sweet moment to me. But I've come to realize that this story is for me. You see, foot washing is part of being a mom, both figuratively and literally. Our children will not always remember everything we said or did, but they are likely to remember being showered with love when they expected something altogether different.

LET'S PRAY

Father, thank You for all the opportunities I have to serve my family. Sometimes I forget that serving translates to loving them. Help me to have Your heart for caring and showing love through daily acts of service. I'm thankful that You set such a beautiful example for loving others. In Jesus' name, Amen.

ACTIVITY

Teach your children to serve their family by helping with chores around the house. Wiping the table after dinner and putting away the dishes helps everyone. Even little ones can help put away their toys after they play. Make serving each other part of your family!

THE STRONGEST LINK

Praise the Lord; praise God our savior!
For each day he carries us in his arms.

Psalm 68:19

When I was in elementary school, we often played a game called "Red Rover." Children would divide into two teams and face each other in lines several yards apart. Team A formed a chain by holding hands and called out to Team B, "Red Rover, Red Rover, let (insert name) come over." The person from Team B whose name was called then ran as fast as he or she could toward Team A and would try to break the chain by targeting who they thought would be the weakest link. I didn't really like this game very much. Because I was small and not very strong, I was often seen as the weakest link. By the time the game was over, my hands and arms were a bit sore. Eventually, though, I learned that if my teammates and I held each other's hands tightly, stood firm, and gave a bit, we weren't going to break our grip when the person ran into us. It would likely be a little uncomfortable, but our hold would remain secure.

Fast forward many years later, I'm married, born again, and preparing to teach a marriage class with my husband at our church. While I was in the process of organizing our notes,

"Red Rover" came to my mind. I realized that the steps that helped me do well in the game could also help couples do well in their marriages.

1. Hold on—to the Lord and to each other.
   It's important to hold on to the Lord first. When He is our anchor, it is easier to hold on to each other.
2. Stand firm—planted in God's Word.
   Many resources claim to be able to help couples through marital crises. Let's be sure that whatever (or whomever) we look to for help is grounded in God's Word. The Bible is true, unwavering, and full of life.
3. Give a little (or a lot)—in humility.
   When we humbly seek understanding and unity with each other, God brings revelation and peace, and we grow stronger and more resilient in our relationship. Is it okay to get upset? Yes. Is it okay to stay upset? No.

We want to work toward a resolution so we can get to a place of harmony. Allow the Lord to be the strongest link in your relationship. His strength is more than sufficient to carry you through anything!

LET'S PRAY

Father, I am so grateful that You can carry my marriage through all the ups and downs of life. Help me walk in humility as I seek to love and serve my husband. When circumstances call for tough discussions, allow me to speak through a heart of love. Thank You for my marriage. In Jesus' name, Amen.

ACTIVITY

How long has it been since you wrote your husband a love letter? Take some time this week to write and tell him how much you love him and how thankful you are for your marriage.

FINDING THE MIDDLE

*May God, who gives this patience and encouragement, help
you live in complete harmony with each other, as is fitting for
followers of Christ Jesus.*

Romans 15:5

I really enjoy decorating and redecorating my home. Can you
relate? Moving things here and there and making sure everything is balanced. Often, I'll place something in the middle of a
shelf and move back a few feet. It looks good to the eye ... until
I actually measure it. Once I use a measuring tape or the width
of my hand, it's easy to see that the object is off center. Finding
the middle in décor placement is easy when you take the time
to measure.

Over the years I've heard some say that when it comes to
disagreements in marriage it's important to meet in the middle.
My thought about that is, *Where's the middle?* Unlike decorating where measuring instruments are used universally, when it
comes to marital issues, middle ground is not easily measured
by any instrument, least of all the human heart.

In the Bible, marriage is seen as a representation of God
and His Bride, the Church (you and me). When I look at the
relationship between God and His Church, there is no middle
ground. God made a way for us to be made sinless when Jesus

came in human form, died on the cross for our sins, and rose again to give us eternal life in heaven. There was no meeting in the middle. Jesus did it all for you and for me. It was completely one-sided—His beautiful and loving side.

Am I saying that one of us should "give in" when there are conflicts? Should one of us always agree to disagree? Should we take turns? No, no, and no.

What I am saying is that seeking middle ground is a good first step. But keep in mind that it's only one step. There will be times when you and your spouse are able to come to agreement in the "middle." I believe, however, that the majority of our marital disagreements will lead to one "giving" a bit more than the other. And that's okay! These moments of surrender and submission on both sides help to make us more Christ-like by putting our spouse before ourselves. Unless you're being asked to do something sinful, immoral, or illegal, compromise can be a good decision when you are both in agreement.

Here's a thought: what if we both sought the Lord? What if we both chose to put Him in the middle—the center—of every conversation? Whether a talk, disagreement, or discussion that requires a decision, if God is at the center, we're sure to come to agreement. Why? Because when He is at the center of your marriage, both of you will have your eyes on Him and what He wants, not on yourselves. That, my friend, is a middle ground we can all aspire to get to every day.

LET'S PRAY

Father, thank You for my marriage and for my husband. As we seek to resolve situations that arise in our relationship, help me see him the way You see him. Help me see Your perspective and not my own. Above all, help us both to have hearts that seek Your will above our own. In Jesus' name, Amen.

ACTIVITY

Whether you've been married one year, 60 years, or somewhere in between, think back to the time you knew you had fallen in love with your man. What are three things that come to mind about him? Write them down and share them with him over a romantic dinner. (Ordering takeout counts as a romantic dinner!)

JOY GIVERS

The joy of the Lord is your strength!

Nehemiah 8:10

Mike and I have been married more than 31 years. We've not reached perfection, but we have discovered that our marriage is worth fighting for no matter what! Along the way we've learned a few things that can help marriages experience the joy that we all want in our relationships.

After going through the list below, have your husband read it. Then talk together about which areas you feel great about and which might need some fine tuning. This is not an exhaustive list. You may have some ideas of your own. Allow these "suggestions" to help you make your marriage more enJOYable!

Share your heart every day. Life gets busy. Make time to talk to each other every day. Pick a time that works for both of you and make it a priority to share your heart. If one of you needs more time to share, make sure to schedule a "talk" date as soon as you can.

Commit to church. Make every effort to attend church services each week and get involved in church activities. This demonstrates your obedience to the Lord and shows your family that He is a priority.

Schedule regular dates. Getting ready for a date with your hubby creates excitement as you look forward to spending time together. If money is tight, trade weeks with another couple and take care of each other's children.

Pray together. Praying together creates both intimacy and a spiritual connection in your marriage that draws hearts together.

Communicate your needs. You don't know what you don't know, so tell each other what's on your mind. Be gentle to share and humble to receive.

Choose to forgive. Forgiveness doesn't always come easily. Depending on the offense, it can take time. If you've caused the situation, sincerely apologize. Be patient as you continue to show your love and care. If you're the offended party, extend forgiveness. This doesn't mean you overlook the circumstances. It means you forgive and agree to move forward. Depending on the situation, there may be a need for Christian counseling. Get help.

Work through conflict. Talk things through. This means letting one person talk while the other listens silently. If you need a break, take time to regroup and then continue to talk things through. If this is a continual occurrence, Christian counseling may be needed.

Listen and learn. It's hard to hear a spouse's heart when the other spouse keeps interrupting. (I may or may not do this sometimes.) Let them share without asking questions or giving clarification. When we allow each other to talk, we are honoring their feelings, and we learn more about them.

Share your vision. What goals do you each have for your marriage? What dreams would you like to see fulfilled in your relationship? Travel, sports, painting, writing, recreational activities ... what is on the horizon?

Speak life. Make it a habit to keep negative talk out of your conversations. Period. That includes not saying anything negative about your spouse or about yourself. Proverbs 18:21 says, "The tongue can bring death or life." Choose life!

Seek godly friendships. It's important to fellowship with other believers. Fun times and memories are made when we do life with friends.

Read God's Word every day. When we commit to get in the Word daily, we are better prepared to tackle whatever life throws at us. God's Word gives us the strength and wisdom we need to live for Him.

Serve each other in love. Jesus came to serve. He set the ultimate example by dying on the cross for our sins. Dying to our own desires isn't easy, but the rewards are huge! When we put our spouse's needs before our own, we are saying that they are the most important person in our lives.

LET'S PRAY

Father, thank You for my husband. He is the perfect gift for my heart. Help me to love him and serve him wholeheartedly. May our marriage reflect Your love for us—unwavering, forgiving, and strong. In Jesus' name, Amen.

ACTIVITY

Think back to your wedding day. Pick one sweet memory of that special time. Write about it in your journal and share that memory with your husband on your next date night.

SECTION 3

THE LITTLE THINGS

And you must love the Lord your God with all your heart, all your soul, and all your strength. And you must commit yourselves wholeheartedly to these commands that I am giving you today. Repeat them again and again to your children. Talk about them when you are at home and when you are on the road, when you are going to bed and when you are getting up. Tie them to your hands and wear them on your forehead as reminders. Write them on the doorposts of your house and on your gates.

Deuteronomy 6:5–9

There are so many ways we can help our children learn about God and how His Son, Jesus, came to bring us salvation. Each day offers new opportunities to share about God's goodness and faithfulness. The Bible, God's Word, gives us wisdom, strength, and everything we need to teach and share with our families about their heavenly Father.

DAY 19

MIND YOUR MANNERS

Don't be selfish; don't try to impress others. Be humble, thinking of others as better than yourselves. Don't look out only for your own interests, but take an interest in others, too.

Philippians 2:3–4

Yes sir! No sir! Yes ma'am! No ma'am! Please and thank you. These words matter. All the time, every day, manners matter. And like everything else we do as parents, our example will go a long way in helping our children be the polite little humans we want them to be.

I remember one time when Jacob was little, I told him to do something. I honestly don't remember what it was, but I was telling him to act on a request. He very nicely responded, "No, thank you." It was the most polite way of disobeying I have ever heard! While he may not have learned at the time to always obey his Mama, he had learned to respond and do so politely. I must say I was very impressed!

During my husband's years as a professional golfer, we were on the road quite a bit. We often ate at restaurants, and it was important for our sons to have good table manners. No food throwing, no kicking under the table, no standing on your chair, no lying on the restaurant floor, etc. These were things we taught them and practiced when we were home. They learned that how we behaved at home or at a restaurant or anywhere else should always be the same. Patience is key, for them and for us as parents. Repetition helps, but giving consistent encouragement is always the best!

Role playing also helped us teach our young boys to remember certain mannerly gestures such as shaking hands when appropriate and looking people in the eye when they are speaking or were spoken to by others. Practicing these things at home made them more comfortable, and eventually these became second nature for them.

When birthdays or gift-giving holidays rolled around, we practiced saying "Thank you" when they received gifts. Mike and I told them that if they received a gift they already had, it wasn't necessary to tell the giver that they didn't need another one. And if for some reason, they received a gift they didn't like, didn't want, or weren't allowed to have, "Thank you" was always the best response. The goal in helping our sons learn to respond nicely was for them to be comfortable and kind, not robotic with their manners.

When it came to "ma'ams" and "sirs," I told them that "yes" and "no" were lonely words that needed a ma'am or sir after them. This helped them remember to keep their yeses and nos from being left alone.

Kind and thoughtful mannerly gestures are important because they honor those around us. Teaching our children the beauty of honor will serve them well all their lives.

LET'S PRAY

Father, may my children and I always recognize that when we honor others with our actions, we bring You honor as well. In Jesus' name, Amen.

ACTIVITY

Ask your children, "How can we honor someone today with a kind gesture?" Sending a drawing or handwritten note (for older children) to a loved one would be a wonderful surprise!

YOU'RE TALLER, BUT I'M STILL MOM

My child, listen when your father corrects you.
Don't neglect your mother's instruction.
What you learn from them will crown you with grace
and be a chain of honor around your neck.

Proverbs 1:8–9

I remember one of the first times I noticed. We were in our garage. Something fell to the ground from something that I was carrying. I leaned over to pick it up at the same time that Jacob leaned over. He beat me to it and handed whatever it was to me. That's when I noticed it. We were eye to eye. Well, that's not quite true. Jacob was just slightly taller than me. He saw it as well. I can't remember what he said, but I do recall what I said to him: "You're taller, but I'm still Mom." The words came out, and I knew that this was a pivotal moment. My son, at 13 years of age, was taller than I was, and he was on the road to manhood. His nearing the "man" stage had nothing to do with his height. It was a recognition that he was growing physically, mentally, and spiritually. Jacob was on his way to becoming a man.

I always knew this day would come—the day you realize your child is no longer little. He or she may not be an adult, but they're definitely on that side of the fence. It's fun, scary, and exciting all at the same time! It's a season where you find yourself wondering and asking yourself so many questions. *Have his dad and I covered every important topic about life? Have we instilled a strong work ethic? Does he know how much we love him?* I can honestly say this side of parenting, we definitely did not cover every single thing that comes to mind.

What we did do was let Jacob know that we loved him and that we believed he could do anything God called him to do. We shared about God's goodness and about salvation through Jesus Christ. We let him know that we would always be there for him. Does this mean he never had any challenging circumstances that he had to work through? No. It means that he knew God could and would help him whenever he called out to Him.

As our children get older (and taller), let's remember that they still need our guidance and support. They may be taller, but they still need to know that we love them and are there for them. For those of us moms who are less than model height, let's remember that it's worth it to get up on our toes to give them a hug!

LET'S PRAY

Father, it really is a joy to see our children grow in stature. As my children grow in age and height, help me see them as You do. Help me offer the guidance and care that they need in every season. May they know how loved and cherished they are in our family. In Jesus' name, Amen.

ACTIVITY

Keep a growth chart for your children. You can use one chart for multiple children and write their names, heights, and dates on the chart over the years. You can also chart the measurements on a wall. Another thing to add to the chart would be goals that are reached such as learning to read, accomplishing a new skill, or anything that's important to your children.

DRIVE TIME IS DIVINE TIME

Don't let anyone think less of you because you are young. Be an example to all believers in what you say, in the way you live, in your love, your faith, and your purity.

1 Timothy 4:12

As our sons got older and became involved in sports and church activities, we found ourselves spending more time in the car as I drove them here and there. I quickly realized that I had a captive audience and a unique opportunity to talk and share our hearts with each other. I referred to these moments as "drive time is divine time." The car provided me with time for talks that we may not have had during the course of our days.

You can start by asking open-ended questions that can lead to conversations and connections. Sometimes it's easier for our children to share what's on their minds when they're looking out the window and not directly at us. Some questions to help you get started might be:

- Who are your closest friends? What do you like about them?
- What is something you really like about yourself?
- How is school going? Is there a class you really like or dislike?
- If you could change anything in your world right now, what would it be?

- When you think about the future, what makes you excited?
- Is there anything I can pray about for you?

You may already know some or most of the answers to these questions, but asking them gives your child a chance to share and shows that you're interested in what they have to say. Listen to their answers and thank your children for sharing with you. Let them know that what they share is safe with you, that it is important, and that it matters to you. This may not be the time to give counsel or direction, but let them know that you're available to talk anytime. If you feel the need to discuss something further or to give feedback, ask the Lord for wisdom. Prayerfully follow up with your children and let them know that it is your desire to help them if needed. Remind them of how much you love them and that you are thankful they trusted you with their hearts.

My sons played competitive tennis from a young age through high school. Mike and I spent many hours listening to them after their tournaments, whether they had wins or losses. We rejoiced with them in their wins, and we shared the sting of loss with them as well. Either way, we wanted them to know that we were always available to listen.

You can make your drive time divine time too! You'll be connecting your hearts with every mile you drive.

LET'S PRAY

Father, I'm thankful that I have so many opportunities to encourage my children every day. Help me to recognize when they need a word of encouragement or some time to talk. May our daily interactions bring our family closer together each day. In Jesus' name, Amen.

ACTIVITY

Make a list of questions you can ask your children when driving them to different activities. Let them know that they can ask you questions as well. Remember that drive time becomes divine time when we connect by sharing our hearts.

BACKGROUND NOISE

I have hidden your word in my heart,
that I might not sin against you.

Psalm 119:11

During a recent visit with the "grands" at our home, Mike and I pulled out some of the toys we had kept from when our sons were little. We thought that one day these playthings would come in handy for future generations, and we were right! One of the toys our grandsons love to play with is a battery-operated piano. It's just the right size for little hands—not too big and not too small. With the press of a button, this melodic treasure plays a few instrumental pieces and continues to play nonstop until you turn it off or the batteries give out. There are also buttons that play different percussion sounds.

I've found that when the toy piano is playing, it's easy to forget that it's even on. The sounds get swallowed up by whatever is happening in the room. Crying babies, conversations, and miscellaneous noises all seem to come together into a swirl of sound. It's what we call background noise. It can become so much a part of our daily happenings that it seems normal. The background noise can become part of daily life, and if we aren't careful, it can drown out the most important voice we need to hear—the voice of God. When we stop listening to His voice, it becomes too easy to stop obeying.

What are some noises that can creep into our minds and hearts? Often they are lies the enemy throws at us, such as "You are unlovable," "You will never succeed," or "You don't matter." The enemy's goal is to make us believe that we have no future. But that is a lie! God loves you. He sees you, and His plans for you are wonderful!

Another source of noise is putting the thoughts of man above the heart of God. There's no doubt that it is good to have godly family and friends who will speak into your life. It's important to have fellowship with other believers who walk with the Lord and give godly counsel. We must always remember, however, that our life choices are ultimately dependent on hearing and obeying God's Word. Yes, He will encourage us and help us through godly loved ones, but the Lord's voice should have the most prominent place in our hearts and minds.

Probably the loudest noise is the worldly belief that we can do everything with our own strength, might, and knowledge. Granted, we may be able to get some things done, but inevitably we will tire physically, mentally, and spiritually if we strive to make things happen ourselves. It is only by God's power and leading that we will walk in the fullness of joy He calls us to live in as moms and women of God. Jesus asked, "What do you benefit if you gain the whole world but lose your own soul?" (Mark 8:36). Let's purpose to get the background noise out of our lives and open our hearts and ears to God's voice in all things.

LET'S PRAY

Father, I desire to keep Your Word in my heart and mind so that I can better hear and recognize Your voice over the noise of this world. When life gets too loud, may Your peace be my refuge, may Your love be my strength, and may Your Word keep me from stumbling. In Jesus' name, Amen.

ACTIVITY

Psalm 119:11 reminds us that when we know God's Word and hold it close, we have the best heart posture for obedience. How can we hide God's Word in our hearts? There are different ways of memorizing Scripture. For example, you can write a verse down several times every day until it sticks in your mind. You can also read and reread a verse until it's easy to repeat. Or you can make a verse part of a prayer so that it comes more naturally to your mind. Whatever you decide to do, know that every memorized verse is part of your spiritual arsenal as you live your Christian life.

DO I HAVE YOUR HEART?

Children are a gift from the Lord;
they are a reward from him.

Psalm 127:3

When my sons were young, I would occasionally ask them, "Do I have your heart?" Mike and I knew there would be a whole world of things, people, attractions, etc. vying for their attention and affection, and we wanted to be the holders of their hearts. It was a priority to be their heart keepers until they surrendered their hearts and lives to Jesus.

To ensure our children's hearts are open to us when they are older, we need to have regular heart connections when they are young. In other words, if we want to be part of their adult world, we need to be present in their childhood world. There will be times when we need to reassess our priorities. It's easy to become involved with so many worthwhile activities outside the home that we can begin to lose footing in our family relationships. We need to ask the Lord, "How do You want me to spend my time?" and then follow His direction.

There was a season when I was very involved with a ministry at our church. One day I asked Jacob, "Do I have your heart?" He told me that I seemed to be spending a lot of time serving in this particular ministry. Sensing he might be right, I talked to

Mike. We prayed and agreed that I would step down. I knew it was the best thing for my family at that time. A few years later, the Lord made a way for me to serve in that ministry again.

As your children get older, there may be times when you feel a shift in the relationship. They're maturing and learning to make some decisions on their own. This is a normal and healthy part of growing up, but it's important to keep those lines of communication open should there be a concern that needs to be addressed.

Situations may arise where we sense or see their hearts pulling away from us. This doesn't always signal a break in the relationship. It may simply mean that they are learning to work things out for themselves. If we have set the example of praying about decisions, then our children will likely do the same. Our job, then, is to continue seeking the Lord in all things and including them in the process. When we do this, we are building on the foundation of trusting God and trusting each other.

Growing up can be hard and confusing for everyone involved. Let your children know they are loved no matter what. Let them know you are always available to talk, to pray, or to sit and be silent together. As your children see the Lord's goodness and faithfulness in your life, they will grow in their desire for Him. Ultimately, the goal of parenthood is to see your children totally surrender their hearts to the Lord.

Developing a strong relationship with our children is all about the heart. When we have their hearts, we're better equipped to help them grow in every area of their lives. Most importantly, when our hearts are connected, we are positioned to help them know and love the Lord.

LET'S PRAY

Father, You have my heart. As I seek to hold the hearts of my children, help me show them Your love in all I do as their mom. May my actions be a godly representation of Your goodness and faithfulness in our lives. I desire to hold their hearts tenderly and lovingly. In Jesus' name, Amen.

ACTIVITY

Ask the Lord how you can hold the hearts of your children. Each one is unique, and how you hold their hearts will be unique to each one as well. Make it a regular part of conversation to ask what they like to do and what activities they enjoy. Keep these ideas in your journal. When one-on-one times are scheduled, you'll have some ideas for your next adventure!

DAY 24

SETTING A GODLY EXAMPLE

And you yourself must be an example to them by doing good works of every kind. Let everything you do reflect the integrity and seriousness of your teaching.

Titus 2:7

We've all heard that behavior is more often caught than taught. In other words, our children are likely to do what we do rather than what we say. It falls on us parents to do what we are asking them to do. For example, if I leave my shoes, books, and papers on the family room floor on a daily basis, I will be hard pressed in asking that my children pick up their things every day. If I have a bad attitude about housework, it's unlikely that my children will look forward to helping around our home. And if I make excuses for not following through on things, it shouldn't surprise me if my children fail to follow through on what I ask of them. Now, the argument is sometimes made, "Well, I'm the parent." Yes, you are, and you (and I) should set the example for them to follow. We can't expect more from our children than we do from ourselves. Everything we do as parents tells them something about our heavenly Father. This isn't meant to scare you; on the contrary, it's meant to motivate all of us to lead by example.

Admit your mistakes. Making a mistake is a great opportunity to show our children that when this happens, we acknowledge what we've done and apologize. I'll never forget the time Mike and I were preparing to teach a class on parenting. I was in the middle of reviewing our notes when one of our sons started asking me questions. I barely responded. He kept talking, and I lost it. "I'm working on a teaching on parenting. Give me some time!" The words flew out of my mouth. I felt terrible. I said, "I'm sorry. I was wrong." Apologizing acknowledges our mistakes and shows our children that no one, not even Mom, always gets it right.

Make the Lord part of your everyday life. When our sons were little, I would intentionally read my Bible where they could see me. I wanted them to know that it was important to me. Mike and I also made prayer a part of our everyday lives. Include your children in your prayer times whenever possible. An easy way to share Jesus with your children is to play praise and worship music at home and in the car. There are many great Christian songs available for every age, and you can also include songs as part of your bedtime routine.

Have grateful attitudes. Being thankful in everyday situations will go a long way in teaching our children the importance of being grateful. Thanking each other for any kindness that is extended to us is a reminder to always thank the Lord for His goodness in our lives. Grateful hearts foster grateful lives, and that's a wonderful example for our families.

Each day we have numerous opportunities to show repentant hearts and demonstrate how important the Lord is to our lives. We can also show gratitude in our day-to-day interactions. Anything we do to show our family that we love and serve the Lord will go a long way in giving them a picture of a godly life.

LET'S PRAY

Father, I pray that my daily life would bring You glory and praise. My hope is that all that I do will be a godly example for my children to follow. May my parenting represent Your loving kindness to my family. In Jesus' name, Amen.

ACTIVITY

What are some things you are already doing to show a godly example to your children? What are some new things you would like to try? Ask the Lord to help you. He knows the best way for you to help your children learn by your example.

THE GIFT OF ENCOURAGEMENT

I pray that God, the source of hope, will fill you completely with joy and peace because you trust in him. Then you will overflow with confident hope through the power of the Holy Spirit.

Romans 15:13

One of the best gifts we can give our children every day is an encouraging word from Scripture. The Bible is full of life-giving verses that can transform our lives with the encouragement they bring to our families. The word "encouragement" is translated *paraklesis* in the Greek, which means 'a calling near.' It's the image of bringing others alongside of you so that you can encourage them as you do life together. This is why the Holy Spirit is sometimes referred to as the Paraclete. He's the One who comes alongside us to exhort and encourage us. It's the Holy Spirit who quickens our spirits with words of life and encouragement for ourselves and for others who may need extra affirmation to help them grow in their walk with the Lord. It's the totality of God's Word and the power of the Holy Spirit that give us the wisdom and strength to speak boldly when needed. Most importantly, God gives us the heart to speak all things in love.

As a mom it's a wonderful blessing to be able to do this with your children every day. And while there are many opportunities to speak life over your littles, it's equally important to recognize those moments when you can encourage the older children and young adults in your family. Adult children need affirmation and encouragement too!

When we encourage our children as the term *paraklesis* implies, we aim to do several things:

- **Exhort**: Encouraging and building others up.
- **Urge**: Lovingly giving that little push that's sometimes needed in their walk with the Lord.
- **Comfort**: Being there when they may fall and helping them get up and keep going; reminding them that we love them and God loves them.

That's what we are all called to do, isn't it? To encourage and love others with the love of God.

Gracious words are a honeycomb,
    sweet to the soul and healing to the bones
    (Proverbs 16:24 NIV).

Prayerfully determine to speak sweet words of life and love over your children, over your marriage, and over every relationship in your life. This is an investment that will pay off in a great return of a loving relationship.

LET'S PRAY

Father, You have set such a beautiful and loving example of bringing encouragement into my life through Your Word and through the people in my life. Thank You for being the voice in my heart that cheers me on as I seek to care for my family. I am grateful to walk alongside You in this journey of being Mom. I love You! In Jesus' name, Amen.

ACTIVITY

Make giving an encouraging word to your family part of your daily life. It could be a Scripture or an encouraging "Way to go!". To help you prepare, write down a list of encouraging verses from the Bible. You'll be armed with life-giving words for your entire family!

DAY 26

OUR TRUSTWORTHY FATHER

Trust in the Lord with all your heart;
do not depend on your own understanding.
Seek his will in all you do,
and he will show you which path to take.

Proverbs 3:5–6

Trust is hard. Not all the time, of course, But sometimes it's hard to trust that all will be well with our children.

When I became a mom, I was sometimes overwhelmed by the enormity of the responsibility. If I didn't feed my children, they wouldn't eat. If I didn't bathe them, they wouldn't be clean. If I didn't hold them and love them, they wouldn't be held or loved. If I didn't, then they wouldn't. It was in these moments that I learned to trust God with everything. He would help me. He would guide me and strengthen me. And guess what? He did. Every. Single. Time.

In those early years when I was feeling tired or inadequate, I trusted God. I'm not saying I never had tough days, because I did. What I am saying is that I realized I wasn't alone. The Lord was with me every step of the way. When I was sad, disappointed, tired, or overwhelmed, I reminded myself to trust God. Every time, every day, it is a choice to trust the Lord and believe the promises in His Word.

As your children get older, pray for them to make godly decisions and choices and trust the Lord to help them. Now that I have adult children who are raising children of their own, I continue to trust Him. He knows the plans for my family. He knows what's best for every season and every situation. It's always a choice, isn't it? I trust Him with today, and then tomorrow I get to choose to trust Him all over again. He's proven Himself faithful every time and every day.

Here's a vision for parenting: every single thing we do, no matter how big or small, should serve to draw our children's hearts into a closer relationship with us and, ultimately, toward the heart of God. As much as we love our children, He loves them even more. His desire is that they walk with Him all the days of their lives.

> If you want favor with both God and man, and a reputation for good judgment and common sense, then trust the Lord completely; don't ever trust yourself. In everything you do, put God first, and He will direct you and crown your efforts with success (Proverbs 3:4–6 TLB).

This verse is for both our children and ourselves. Trust God to give you wisdom as you parent your little ones and your big ones. Give God access to every area of your life. Let me encourage you to be fearless in setting culturally unpopular boundaries for your family. The Lord does not concern Himself with popularity, and neither should we. Believe God's Word for your loved ones. Our Father's concern is always for the health of our hearts and our relationship with Him. So it is with the relationship we desire for our children, regardless of their ages.

LET'S PRAY

Father, I am so glad I can trust You for every area of my life. You always show Yourself faithful. And when I don't understand what's happening, I trust that You will guide my steps. Thank You for always being worthy of my love and my trust. In Jesus' name, Amen.

ACTIVITY

Ask yourself, *What do I need to trust God with today?* During your quiet time, recall the times He has proven Himself faithful. Write them down in your journal. This will help you remember that God is always worthy of your trust.

DAY 27

PASSION

Work willingly at whatever you do, as though you were working for the Lord rather than for people.

Colossians 3:23

D o you ever have the feeling that you're "just a mom"? Your thoughts turn to wondering if you'll ever have the opportunity to carry out the passions that are on your heart. It's not that you don't love being mom, it's just that ... well, what if someone else starts doing what you wanted to do and now you can't do it because they did it already?! What if someone else starts that business or writes that book? Yes, those thoughts can ruin a perfectly great life of motherhood *if* we let them take hold of our minds and hearts.

I believe passion is a gift from God that is perfectly tailored for each one of us. The word passion comes from the Latin *pati,* which means 'to endure or to suffer.' This is what is meant by the passion of Christ. It refers to the suffering of our Lord. Today, the word passion is primarily used to mean having a strong and uncontrollable emotion and/or conviction that is usually associated with love. Put these two descriptions together, and you have what I call the Lord's passion: a strong, unchanging, and never-ending love for us that led Jesus to the cross where He endured great suffering and died. Then He rose again so that we, His bride, could spend eternity with Him in heaven. That's passion!

> Delight yourself in the Lord
> and he will give you the desires of your heart
> (Psalm 37:4 ESV).

I love this verse because it assures us that when we delight in our Lord by seeking His heart through praying, getting in the Word, and spending time in worship, our hearts will align with His. Our desires will become the desires He has for us. If you have a passion that's stirring in your heart, take that desire to the Father. Allow Him to speak to your heart through His Word and through godly counsel if needed. If the Lord has given you a desire to serve in a ministry or to start a business or (insert your desire), then realize that it's all in His timing. He does not tease us with the dreams and desires we have inside us. The Lord may release you to move forward even with a growing family, or He may have you wait until sometime down the road.

Remember, the best place to be is where God has called us to be. Rest in that and find joy in whatever place you find yourself. I didn't have my first book published until I was 59. Could I have written it earlier? Yes. Would it have been the same book? No. God's timing was perfect for me, and it is for you too. Only He knows the when and the how of whatever may be on your horizon.

If you're in the waiting season, use it to learn and grow in Him. Although you may know what your heart is drawn to, there may be no open doors in the area of your passion. If this is your situation, know that God will use whatever is happening in your season of waiting. God wastes nothing. Most importantly, always remember that our God-given passions, while they may be fun or exciting, are ultimately for His people and His glory.

I firmly believe that being Mom gives you the most important audience you'll ever have—your children. Each day you have the opportunity to help mold them into men and women who will love and serve the Lord wholeheartedly. That's a passion that we can all aspire to have in our hearts.

LET'S PRAY

Father, thank You for my family. I'm so grateful for this season of being Mom. When my heart yearns to do more for Your Kingdom, remind me that I am helping raise Kingdom builders here at home. Knowing that your timing is perfect, I will continue to seek Your face as I look forward to walking in all the passions You have lovingly placed on my heart. In Jesus' name, Amen.

ACTIVITY

Study the word passion and share it with your children. Together, you can pray and ask the Lord what passions He may have for each of you. Write them down and review them every couple months. Continue seeking the Lord together. This is a great way for you, your husband, and your children to share what God is showing each of you. It also gives your family members an opportunity to pray for each other about their possible future callings.

INTENTIONAL INVESTMENTS

Direct your children onto the right path,
and when they are older, they will not leave it.

Proverbs 22:6

B eing parents gives us the incredible responsibility of helping our children move "onto the right path." There are numerous commentaries regarding this verse, but the common denominator is that as parents, we see our child's strengths and gifts and can encourage them as they begin thinking about their future callings.

Together, with our children, we want to seek God's heart for their lives. Let them know from an early age that you are praying for them. As they get older and begin to think seriously about their future callings, remind them that you are there for them, you support them, and you are always available to talk. If they ask for your opinion, then you have an open door to share your heart with them. We want to create an atmosphere where you can express your thoughts without making your maturing children feel controlled. When they feel loved, heard, and understood, they are much more receptive to input.

From the day our children enter the world, our number one responsibility is to help lead them to the saving grace of Jesus Christ. As our children grow up, we will have numerous opportunities to talk about God and His love for us. We'll also begin to see their own unique traits.

Both of our sons were joyful babies and enjoyed playing together. Mike and I could already see their giftings emerging when they were young. Even as a little boy, Jacob loved to write. He wrote a little book and illustrated it as well. Today, he is a full-time writer. Joel was always discerning and detail oriented. He works in a job that requires much detailed work, and his discernment contributes to his ability to get things organized.

When you watch your young children playing and talking, you will likely pick up on some of their talents. Here are a few ways to help you identify their strengths:

- **Pray**—Ask the Lord to show you your children's strengths.
- **Observe**—What do your children like to do? In what areas do they excel?
- **Listen**—What do your children like to talk about? What are they interested in at this time?
- **Encourage**—Be their cheerleader! Let them know you're in their corner.

If you're reading this and thinking, *I don't see any particular strengths right now* or *I see too many things right now*, then please don't worry. Enjoy the process. God's timing is always right. Prayerfully continue to seek His heart for your children and for yourself. The Lord will give you everything you need as you "direct your children onto the right path."

LET'S PRAY

Father, I am so thankful for my children. It's such a blessing to see them growing up and learning so many new things. Help me to recognize those areas that need direction. Help me to encourage those things that You desire for them. I'm grateful that You have a plan for their lives. There is peace in knowing that You love them (and me) so much! In Jesus' name, Amen.

ACTIVITY

What strengths do you see in your children today? What areas need more direction? Pray for both. Ask the Lord to give you wisdom and discernment as you help lead your children into their future callings.

SECTION 4

BEING MOM

The Lord is my strength and shield.
  I trust him with all my heart.
He helps me, and my heart is filled with joy.
  I burst out in songs of thanksgiving.

                                        Psalm 28:7

There are no perfect moms, but we serve a perfect God who can and will help us in all we do. Trust Him to help you be the mom He's called you to be for your children.

DAY 29

THE PERFECT MOM

God arms me with strength,
and he makes my way perfect.

Psalm 18:32

oon after our first son was born, it happened. I was a bit sleep deprived and trying to get things organized at home while making sure Jacob was happy and fed. I walked into our bedroom, and the radio was playing a program with a well-known Christian author and speaker. (Yes, we actually listened to radios in the 90s.) He was saying that the most important person in a young son's life is his mother. *What?* I sat on the edge of the bed and started crying. It was the ugly crying where you can't control the sobs. Mike came in and found me falling apart. All I could think was, *God, what were You thinking? How will I ever be able to be a good mom? My poor son. How am I going to do this?* These may not have been my exact words, but they come pretty close. Mike lovingly reminded me that with God's help we would all be just fine. He was right.

If you were to ask 100 different people how they would define the "perfect" mom, I can pretty much guarantee you would receive 100 different definitions. That's because everyone looks at motherhood differently. One person may say a perfect mom is someone who is always happy and smiling. Another may say it's the mom who keeps her house spotless. Yet another may say it's the mom who seems to have the best-behaved children. Personally, I think the perfect mom is a combination of things only God can determine for each woman. That's because we are each as unique as our children. As Christian moms, our common motherhood denominator is loving Jesus and seeking His wisdom and guidance for our family. Each child is born with a set of traits, strengths, and weaknesses that are his or hers alone, and as moms, we have the privilege of seeking these out while we also seek God's heart for our sons and daughters.

When I began my mothering journey, my prayer was that all I said and did would ultimately bring my children closer to the Lord. I was not—and am still not—a perfect mom, but I certainly do love being a mom. Every season has been a blessing. The Lord gave me such a desire and joy for motherhood that my heart is to encourage other moms on their journeys.

I wish I could tell you that everything I have ever done as a mom was right, that my sons never had any struggles, and that they always obeyed immediately with smiles on their faces. But that would not be true. What I can tell you is that Jacob and Joel have grown to know and love God, know His love for them, know that He has a plan for their lives, and know that they are deeply and unconditionally loved by the Father, Mike, and me. We're parents who have loved their children and desired to follow God's Word to help us help them become all He called them to be. And although we missed the parenting mark at times, our missteps in no way alter what the Bible has to say:

The faithful love of the Lord never ends!
    His mercies never cease.
Great is his faithfulness;
    his mercies begin afresh each morning
    (Lamentations 3:22–23).

God's Word is always true. God's ways are always perfect, always right, and always working for our good. God's love is always faithful and never-ending. And, thankfully, God's mercies are always new every day for our children and for us as parents. Can I hear an Amen?

While none of us will ever get it right all the time, the authority and truth of God's Word are never in question. He was, He is, and He will always be perfect in all His ways.

LET'S PRAY

Father, I'm so grateful that You are always there to give me the wisdom I need to be a mom. Some days are tough, but I know I can always count on You to give me strength and to help me see the joy in every situation. I'm not perfect, but I am the perfect mom for my children. In Jesus' name, Amen.

ACTIVITY

Write down all the things you feel great about being a mom in the season you are in right now. If you can't think of anything, ask the Lord to show you. Then thank Him for these victories!

LOVE OVERCOMES FEAR

For God has not given us a spirit of fear and timidity, but of power, love, and self-discipline.

2 Timothy 1:7

P *arenting.* This word can bring both joy and fear to moms and dads alike. Why? Well, I think it's because the enemy wants us to be fearful *for* our children and fearful *of* our children. He wants us to be fearful that we won't know what to do, that we're going to mess up, and that our days are going to be really, really hard.

Let me make something very clear: we are *not* always going to know what to do. We are going to mess up sometimes. Our little ones and not so little ones are going to be really, really hard work, because bringing up children to know, love, and obey God is a full-time job! With that said, let me make something else very clear: your children will bring you tremendous joy. They are going to help you become a stronger Christian as you get on your knees in prayer for wisdom, strength. and peace. They are going to help you hear the voice of God as you seek Him for counsel. Best of all, they are going to help you fall more deeply in love with the Father as you seek His heart for your family.

Seeking God's heart is a daily discipline. Like everything else we do to keep physically strong and healthy, the daily pursuit of the Lord will give us the supernatural strength and godly wisdom we need as Christian women and moms. God's guidance will enable us to make the ongoing decisions that parenting our children requires of us. When we choose to rely on the Lord, our choices will be determined by following Him and His ways.

Our heavenly Father will always be there for us because He cares for us. First Peter 5:7 instructs us, "Give all your worries and cares to God, for he cares about you."

LET'S PRAY

Father, thank You for my children. Thank you that You love them and that You love me too! When my days are long and my sleep is short, help me focus on You and Your love. I truly have nothing to fear, because my hope is in You! In Jesus' name, Amen.

ACTIVITY

Reflect on God's love for you as His daughter. Write down what the Lord impresses on your heart about His love for you. When you're done, write your heavenly Father a letter of love and thanksgiving.

BYE BYE DISCOURAGEMENT

And this same God who takes care of me will supply all your needs from his glorious riches, which have been given to us in Christ Jesus

Philippians 4:19

One thing I noticed early on as a mom was the discouragement that many parents feel. Mike and I talked about this and asked ourselves two questions:

1. Why do so many parents find themselves discouraged?
2. Why do so many Christian parents find themselves discouraged?

We realized the answer to both questions is the same. Many of us don't read the Bible, or we only read it when we desperately need it. Consequently, we don't know that God has given us so much wisdom and encouragement in His Word.

> Joyful are people of integrity,
>> who follow the instructions of the Lord.
> Joyful are those who obey his laws
>> and search for him with all their hearts (Psalm 119:1–2).

Discouragement is defeated when we surrender control to the Lord. He is available 24 hours a day to help us. His desire is that we joyfully come to Him with all our concerns regarding our children, our marriages, and our lives. Because there's so much information readily available to us, it's important that whatever we read, see, or hear is received in light of what God has to say. Be cautious that you do not allow human opinions to have more authority in your life than God's Word. The authority of the Bible is the ultimate test for determining truth.

Your children will bring you tremendous joy. They will help you learn to hear God's voice as you seek Him for counsel and direction. They will help grow your faith as you pray, asking for wisdom and strength. When you see their faces and your heart swells with love for them, it will serve as a reminder of how much God loves them and you! That alone will fill you with courage as you parent your children.

LET'S PRAY

Father, I'm thankful that discouragement doesn't have to be part of my life. I may get tired and feel overwhelmed at times, but I know that You are the Lord of my life. In the midst of busyness, I just need to remember to turn to You. I'm so glad that You are always there for me and my family. In Jesus' name, Amen.

ACTIVITY

What are some areas or situations that bring up feelings of discouragement? Write them down and prayerfully surrender them to the Lord. Allow Him to minister to your heart in these areas. Anytime you're feeling discouraged, remember to go to the Father for a fresh filling of His strength and love.

DAY 32

IT'S NOT A RACE

I press on to reach the end of the race and receive the heavenly prize for which God, through Christ Jesus, is calling us.
Philippians 3:14

Mike was a professional golfer when our sons were born, and he continued in this profession throughout their early childhood. We traveled as a family all over the country and stayed at countless hotels during this season. One thing that many hotels have in common are elevators. Our young sons would run to the elevator to see who would get there first. Being the older one, Jacob was usually the first to arrive and push the up or down button. This was followed by the younger Joel, responding, "Jacob, it's not a race." He said this with the cutest three-year-old voice, adding as much authority as he could muster.

When I think of this, I'm reminded that parenting is sometimes seen as a race. The enemy would have us believe that our children are a bother and a barrier to enjoying life. Moms and dads may be racing to reach an invisible finish line where kids are grown and out of the house. Sadly, others may believe they're supposed to suffer through parenting, so they want to get through it as quickly as possible. In the famous words of Joel, "It's not a race." While parenting can definitely be challenging and tiring, it is not something to hurry through.

I do believe it's important to encourage children to grow, mature, and seek God's plan for their future. As parents, we can absolutely enjoy the process of helping them develop their strengths and abilities. However, it's also important to recognize and celebrate each season with our young ones. Let's not mentally rush them out the door. Every phase of life brings new opportunities for encouragement, training, and connection. Perhaps the one thing your heart needs to hear today is this: *you can enjoy life right now with your children.* Yes, there may be situations that test your parenting resolve. There are likely going to be ages and stages where your children will help enhance your prayer life. Still, I can assure you that with God's help, you can treasure family moments throughout the years. Your children will eventually leave home one day, and you will be grateful for the precious time you had to lay a strong foundation of love and faith in their lives.

Today's verse speaks of reaching the end of the race. This is the race we all have, parents and children alike. Unlike a race for a political position or any "thing" else, it's the race within ourselves to choose daily whether we live for God or for ourselves. Let's purpose to choose wisely and set a godly example for our children in every season.

LET'S PRAY

Father, I want to fully enjoy each stage of my children's lives. Help me see beyond the challenges. Give me eyes to see the everyday moments as an opportunity to make sweet memories. In Jesus' name, Amen.

ACTIVITY

Ask the Lord what you can do today to make a fun family memory. Make it a regular prayer to ask Him and write down every idea He gives you in your journal.

MY MOM VERSE

Rejoice always, pray continually, give thanks in all circumstances; for this is God's will for you in Christ Jesus.

1 Thessalonians 5:16–18 (NIV)

I must have read this Scripture many times before, but one day, it really spoke to my mama's heart. I knew that I wanted it to be my life Scripture for being Mom.

"Rejoice always." Always? Even when I'm exhausted from being up most of the night for the fifth day in a row? Yes. Even when the baby has his days and nights mixed up? Yes. Even when I'm feeling a bit overwhelmed? Yes. When the Lord inspired the apostle Paul to write "always," He meant it! How do we do it? How do we maintain a "rejoice always" mentality? Just as a lamp won't turn on unless the cord gets plugged into the electrical outlet, we must plug our hearts into the Source of joy—God. It's not always easy, but I believe the Lord wants us to know that it's always possible through Him.

"Pray continually." In other words, pray all the time for everything. As I wrote this, the thought came to me, *What if I prayed instead of complained?* Wow! It could just be me, but when things aren't going as I like or when I'm feeling stressed, my human tendency is to whine about it. "Why is this happening? How do I fix it? Can somebody please do something NOW?!" But if I chose to pray instead, my heart rate would surely stay steadier. My focus wouldn't be on whatever is stressing me out; it would be on the Lord. Most importantly, I'd be going to the only One who can bring peace and joy to any and all situations.

"Give thanks in all circumstances." We're called to give thanks in all circumstances, not just when things are going well. Even when things are downright ugly, we're called to give thanks. Why? Because regardless of whatever we may go through, God is always there to help us get through the situation. In the driest seasons and in the darkest times of loss, I can testify that God has brought His peace and love into every single moment. We can give thanks because when we allow Him into our sadness and pain, He brings His healing and restoration. It's not always easy to walk through difficulties, but His presence makes it doable, and for that we can always be thankful.

This is my Mom Verse. Do you have one? You're welcome to make this your verse too! But first, I suggest that you seek the Father's heart. He knows you best and has a verse that will encourage you. It may be the same verse I have, or He may have another one that is just for you.

LET'S PRAY

Father, thank You that Your Word brings life and wisdom to every situation that may arise in my life. I'm grateful that You are always there for me and that You have given me the gift of being Mom. May Your Word continue to guide me and help me in this motherhood journey. In Jesus' name, Amen.

ACTIVITY

Once you have your Mom Verse, write it down where you can see it every day. Before you know it, you'll have it memorized and planted in your heart. What a sweet gift from the Father!

DAY 34

PERFECT LOVE

But you are to be perfect, even as your Father in heaven is perfect.
Matthew 5:48

This verse can seem quite daunting. However, in this context, "perfect" doesn't mean flawless or without sin, because that's impossible for any human. We all make mistakes. Perfect in this verse means "finished, complete, pure, holy." When we are born again, God makes us complete through His Son, our Lord Jesus. He gives us the power to love people like He does— wholly, unconditionally, and unendingly.

This perfect love is not contingent on having to be a "perfect" mom. Your words and actions will have a much greater impact on your children than a decorated house, designer clothing, or expensive toys. Ask the Lord to show you His heart for your children and for the people in your life. Choose to love them as God loves you.

I once spoke with a woman who was experiencing a difficult situation with her adult child. She was frustrated and overwhelmed, and she questioned every parenting decision she had ever made. As a mom I understood her pain and confusion. I've experienced the same doubts and felt the same sting of inadequacy.

While she spoke, the Lord gave me a wonderful picture of encouragement to share. I said, "None of us get 'being Mom' perfectly." I asked her to imagine making a list of all the things she believed she had done wrong. Then I said, "Imagine the hand of God dipping a huge paint brush at the foot of the cross where the blood of Jesus was flowing down. See the Lord taking that blood-soaked brush and swiping it up and down over that list of mistakes." I went on to encourage her that all our past, current, and future failings are covered by the blood of Jesus.

Every mom (including me!) needs to hear that encouragement and anchor it in her heart. Motherhood can be hard sometimes, and so can life in general. Sickness. Rebellion. Drugs. Pornography. Anger. Divorce. Death. The list goes on and on. Whatever your situation may be, God is there for you, and His love for you is never-ending. May the words of the apostle Paul bring hope and healing to your heart:

I am convinced that nothing can ever separate us from God's love. Neither death nor life, neither angels nor demons, neither our fears for today nor our worries about tomorrow—not even the powers of hell can separate us from God's love. No power in the sky above or in the earth below—indeed, nothing in all creation will ever be able to separate us from the love of God that is revealed in Christ Jesus our Lord (Romans 8:38–39).

LET'S PRAY

Thank You, Father, that You are a constant source of love and strength. Even in those days or weeks or seasons when circumstances may be difficult, I can rest assured that You will always be there for me. Nothing can ever separate me from Your love. In Jesus' name, Amen.

ACTIVITY

Do you have a list of those things that make you feel inadequate as a mom? Your heavenly Father sees you and loves you unconditionally. Make a mental list of three to five things that you believe you need to improve. Take them to the Lord in prayer and ask Him to help you. Then go to the Scriptures and find some encouraging verses that show how God sees you. For example, Psalm 139:14 says you are "fearfully and wonderfully made" (NIV), and Philippians 4:13 says, "I can do everything through Christ, who gives me strength." Be encouraged! God is always there for you!

DAY 35

THAT'S A THOUGHT!

So let us come boldly to the throne of our gracious God. There we will receive his mercy, and we will find grace to help us when we need it most.

Hebrews 4:16

It's amazing how many unsolicited ideas, tips, and pieces of advice people will give us as women, wives, moms, and humans in general. While some of the information given is well intentioned, it can still be a bit overwhelming, especially to a new mom. With all that said, allow me to give you some advice ... lovingly, of course! When someone says something that you know won't work for you, doesn't fit your personality, or just makes your eyes roll, simply and kindly say, "That's a thought!"

Here are a few reasons why this response is always a winner:

- First, this phrase is perfect because it's true. What they've said is a thought. It may not be your thought, but it is, nonetheless, a thought.
- Second, this phrase isn't committing you to anything. You aren't saying "Yes! I'll try that!" You are just saying that it is a thought—no more and no less.
- Third, should the person who gave you the advice ever ask if you've tried it, you can reply, "I'm still giving it some

thought" or "I still haven't given it some thought." Either way you're being truthful.

The best thing about these responses is that they are honest. Now, if the person asks if you like their idea or plan on implementing their counsel, you can just say, "I'll have to plan to give it some more thought!" The only downside to all this is that at some point you may actually need to think about it and simply say, "That didn't work for us."

Disclaimer: When it comes to our children and their ideas, a simple yes or no is always best. If you tell them you're going to think about it, then you'll need to think about it and tell them your decision.

Another Disclaimer: If I know you and you have given me some ideas and I responded, "That's a thought," thanks for sharing, and I'll think about it. Really!

All kidding aside, there will be advice that is helpful and works well for you, and there will be some that doesn't fit your family well. The best response is always a loving, "That's a thought. Thanks so much for sharing!"

LET'S PRAY

Father, thank You for giving us friends and family who love us and sincerely want to help us. When we find ourselves in situations where we know what is being offered isn't a good fit for our family, give us wisdom to respond with a thankful and loving heart. In Jesus' name, Amen.

ACTIVITY

If your children are old enough, talk to them about the importance of being kind and respectful to those who offer ideas that don't fit your family. While a "That's a thought" response won't necessarily work every time, "Thanks for sharing that thought!" is always a good replacement.

SETTLE DOWN

The teaching of your word gives light,
so even the simple can understand.

Psalm 119:130

When my sons were around three and five years old, I had a habit of telling them to "settle down" when they were getting a little rambunctious. Sometimes I had to tell them more than once! My goal was for them to learn to obey the first time they were told, but when it came to settling down, that was rarely the case.

During this season, we had moved to Texas from Florida. Mike and I were busy doing all the logistical things one has to do when you move to a new town. This particular day we were opening our new bank account. As we talked to the bank attendant, Jacob and Joel sat near us. Before long they were talking and laughing, which was great, but then they got a little loud and a bit distracting. I promptly gave them the "settle down" look. This was followed by my serious "settle down" voice. There was no change in their behavior. In fact, they seemed even happier and were having a great time.

Immediately, I heard the Lord speak to my heart: "Do they know what 'settle down' means?" I thought to myself, *Well, sure they do. I tell them regularly. They must know ... right?*

As they sat nearby giggling, I looked over and asked, "Boys, do you know what 'settle down' means?" Without hesitation, Jacob looked up, smiled, and said, "No ma'am." What?! No wonder they hadn't responded to my "settle downs"! They had no idea what I was talking about. I was asking them to obey, but I hadn't taken the time to explain what obedience looked like in this situation. I smiled and told them to please sit quietly. They understood. We finished our meeting with the banker and headed home.

That day I learned that what we say may make sense to us, but it may not mean anything to our littles. No matter how many times we say something, if they don't understand, they can't obey. As I think back on this day, I'm reminded that when I started my Christian walk with the Lord, I knew very little of what the Bible said about living life. Every time I read it, I learned new things. Most importantly, I learned God's heart for me and what He says about living a life of obedience to Him. Ultimately, we are called to obedience to His Word, and this brings blessings to our lives.

The beauty of this is that the more we read His Word, the more we grow in our walk with Him and the more we grow to know and love our heavenly Father. We learn. We grow. We love. We obey. We are all His children.

My sons did learn to "settle down," and so did I! My heart is settled in God.

LET'S PRAY

Father, thank You for Your patience with me. I don't always understand obedience, but I want to learn. Help me to help my children learn to obey. I know obedience brings blessing, and I pray my children's lives will overflow with blessing upon blessing. In Jesus' name, Amen.

ACTIVITY

Take some index cards and write a few words on each one describing different situations in which you would like to see your children better understand obedience. Have one of your children pick a card each day

SECTION 5

STAYING STRONG

For I can do everything through Christ, who gives me strength.
Philippians 4:13

S ome days can seem longer than others, can't they? One day you've got it all figured out, and then the next day you find that you need a whole new plan! Thankfully, our Father knows the beginning from the end. He has everything we need to get us through every day and every season of being Mom!

DON'T GIVE UP

He gives power to the weak
and strength to the powerless.

Isaiah 40:29

G od's Word stands the test of time over and over again. Living and active, it gives us the strength we need for today and for all our tomorrows.

Here's an acronym to help us in every season of being Mom:

STRENGTH

Stay in the Word.

Take time to reflect on what the Lord is showing you as you pray and read Scripture.

Rest in His presence through worship and prayer.

Energize yourself by eating well and getting proper exercise. See a professional if needed.

Neglect what isn't important. "No" is a good word for those things that are not a priority in your life. Your priorities should be in the following order: God, spouse, children, everything else. (Realistically, when your baby needs something, you obviously need to be there. Babies do change the order of things for a short season.)

Give your time and energy to those things the Lord directs you to do. There will always be wonderful ministries and organizations to be a part of, but seek God's heart first.

Tidy up for 10 minutes a few times a day.

Hug your spouse and your children every day!

LET'S PRAY

Father, thank You that You will always give me strength to do those things You have called me to do. Give me wisdom and direction each day as I seek to do Your will as Your daughter, as a wife, and as a mom. In Jesus' name, Amen.

ACTIVITY

What do your days look like on a regular basis? Are you able to do those things that you would like to get done, such as reading your Bible, finishing a load of laundry, or getting outside for a walk? If your days are filled yet you feel like you aren't accomplishing anything, remember that being Mom involves many things that may not be on a list. Instead of making a list of daily "to dos," try making a list of "did dos." Briefly write the things you got done that day. Thank God for His help. You'll find that you're really rocking it!

WHAT'S ON THE INSIDE?

Each of you should use whatever gift you have received to serve others, as faithful stewards of God's grace in its various forms.
1 Peter 4:10 (NIV)

I was putting on a jacket one morning and noticed something I had never seen. There were large, deep pockets on both sides. Now this is one of my favorite jackets that I wear regularly, yet I didn't know these pockets existed. I had never noticed them before as they were tucked away, but here they were, having been found quite by accident. Interestingly, I found that these pockets could hold a whole lot more than the more obvious ones on the front of the jacket.

Immediately, I felt the Lord encourage my heart. We may sometimes think that we don't have much to offer, but the Lord would have us look inside ourselves. He has deposited His life, His love, and His power in you! As a daughter of the King, you can draw these out from the deep treasure trove we have as His children.

I was reminded of a time when I was preparing to teach a class at our church about motherhood. I asked Jacob if he could give me three words that stood out to him about my mothering. He paused for a bit, and I wondered what he might be thinking. Then he said, "Ability, authentic, and authority." I was overwhelmed. I took his three words and wrote this:

Ability/Capability: We can be the moms God has called us to be for *our* children. I wasn't called to be anybody else's mom. I was uniquely designed to be the mom for the children the Lord brought into my life.

Authentic Christianity: We can each be the woman of God that He designed with the gifts and strengths that are unique to each one of us. These are to be used for His glory!

Authority in Christ: In the name of Jesus, we have the authority to pray the big prayers, to believe for the miraculous, and to walk in victory! Every prayer will not always be answered the way we would like, but we have the assurance that "God causes everything to work together for the good of those who love God and are called according to his purpose for them" (Romans 8:28).

LET'S PRAY

Father, thank You for all You have done and continue to do in my life. Help me to remember that You have given me deep pockets filled with wonderful gifts like strength and wisdom that come from You. Better yet, they will never run out! You are always for me. In Jesus' name, Amen.

ACTIVITY

Ask God what is in the deep pockets of your life. How can these gifts help you as a woman, wife, and mother? Write what He tells you in your journal.

FLIP THE SWITCH

I have come as a light to shine in this dark world, so that all who put their trust in me will no longer remain in the dark.

John 12:46

Years ago, I worked as a writer and photographer. My responsibilities included not only taking pictures but also printing them in a darkroom. There's a reason it's called a darkroom—it's really, really dark. The "can't see your hand in front you" kind of dark. It's necessary to be in total darkness because if light touches the film, the images are ruined and completely erased.

In total darkness, I learned how to remove the film from my camera, roll it onto a reel, and get the reel into a canister. Then the canister had to be closed perfectly so as to not allow any light inside once the light was turned back on. Over time it became fairly easy to work in my darkroom.

Thinking back, it strikes me that many of us live our lives in the dark. It may not be that we live our whole life hidden, but perhaps we've learned to have a darkroom in our hearts where we keep certain things hidden. These may include fear, insecurity, anger, past hurts, or any number of things that we keep closed tightly in our personal canisters.

My friend, if that's you, Jesus desires to bring His light into every area of your life. There is nothing for which He can't bring

His healing, love, and peace to replace the darkness. The light of Jesus will illuminate our lives, enabling us to see more clearly what areas need His healing. The light of Jesus will strengthen our hearts to face those areas that need to be realigned with His best for our lives. The light of Jesus will bring intimacy with the heart of our Savior. When we close any part of ourselves off in the dark, we leave no room for God to work in us.

> For you were once darkness, but now you are light in the Lord. Live as children of light (Ephesians 5:8 NIV).

Knowing who we are in Christ makes all the difference. Over the years I've struggled with fear and insecurity. Fear of failure or making mistakes led to being insecure about so many things in my life. Motherhood certainly brought on more insecurities. What if I did something wrong? What if my children misbehaved? What if they got hurt? The "what ifs" were overwhelming! Once I recognized what was happening, I realized that as I spent time in God's Word, my heart and mind were strengthened, and I was able to take all my insecurities and concerns to the foot of the cross. I was learning to fully trust the Lord for everything in my life! The light of Jesus was lifting the darkness. His light was erasing how I saw myself so that I could have the picture of who He says I am.

When the lies of the enemy try to bring doubt or discouragement, God's Word reminds us, "I am fearfully and wonderfully made" (Psalm 139:14 NIV).

Let's continually open every part of our hearts and lives to the love of Jesus and allow His light to overcome the darkness.

LET'S PRAY

Father, I am so grateful that You love me unconditionally. Thank You that not only are my children "fearfully and wonderfully made," but I am too, because I am Your daughter. Show me, Lord, if there are any areas that need to be brought into the light. I wholeheartedly welcome the light of Jesus into every area of my life. In Jesus' name, Amen.

ACTIVITY

Grab a cup of coffee or tea and your journal and ask the Lord if there are any areas of your life that need the light turned on. Are there hurts that need healing? Have you felt the need for validation? Whatever is weighing on your heart, take it to the Lord in prayer and allow Him to bring His love and healing into the situation. If you need counsel, reach out for help at your nearest church or Christian counseling center.

ONE LITTLE THING

And this same God who takes care of me will supply all your needs from his glorious riches, which have been given to us in Christ Jesus.

Philippians 4:19

I was getting things ready at our home for a small gathering of friends and family. I had pulled out a favorite tablecloth, but as I placed it on the old wooden table, I saw that a small part of the cloth had gotten caught on a splinter of wood. I could see that the material was starting to wrinkle, and the thread was starting to pull. It appeared that a tear was about to happen. Oh no! What would I do now? It was the perfect size for this table, and I had no replacement. I made a quick decision to gently stretch the tablecloth. Ever so softly I stretched. Unbelievably, the wrinkled cloth began to look smooth. No loose threads. There were no signs of the piece having gotten snagged and possibly unraveling. All was well, and peace was restored.

Have you ever gotten snagged? Have you ever gotten in a "mom moment" where things seemed to be slowly then quickly unraveling? What started out as a normal day ends up getting caught in a splinter of sorts, and your mind, heart, and spirit began to feel as if you were falling apart. I don't know of a mom who has never experienced this sense of unraveling—myself included!

It doesn't have to be a huge event either. It could be just one little thing after another after another. Before you know it, the unraveling has begun. The baby is fussy for no apparent reason, the toddler won't eat anything except crackers, your young child decides he doesn't want to use the potty anymore, etc. What to do? Stretch gently. Stretch your heart and remember that God is with you in all the little things that come at you each and every day. He is only a prayer away from you and your family. When God is at the forefront of all you do, unraveling is never an option. Yes, things can and will go wrong at times, but we can be sure that our Father will see us through every single time! He not only unravels our situations, but He can also prevent them from "pulling" at us in the first place.

LET'S PRAY

Father, You know that sometimes my days feel so hectic and out of control. I can easily feel like I'm in a tailspin. Help me remember that You are always there for me. All I need to do is call on You, and You will hear me and bring your peace to the situation. I'm so grateful to know that You are always near and that as Your child, I am always on Your heart. In Jesus' name, Amen.

ACTIVITY

Make a list of those things and situations that tend to cause stress for you. Surrender each stressor to the Lord. Whenever one of these things comes up in your day, remember that you've got this because God has got you!

DON'T MISS OUT

Be shepherds of God's flock that is under your care, watching over them—not because you must, but because you are willing, as God wants you to be; not pursuing dishonest gain, but eager to serve; not lording it over those entrusted to you, but being examples to the flock.

1 Peter 5:2–3 (NIV)

Before Mike and I were parents, we had already prayerfully made the decision to homeschool our children. We wanted to be the biggest influence in their lives, and for our family, that meant being their primary teachers. When we started schooling our sons, we didn't know that we would end up homeschooling through high school. We just knew that God would direct us to do whatever He wanted us to do. Once they were older, we found classes for homeschooled students where they could learn upper-level math, science, and other subjects.

When we began our homeschooling journey, I never let on that I didn't like certain subjects. I didn't want my personal preference to keep my sons from learning and enjoying what they were studying. My thinking was that they would decide for themselves what interested them most in their studies.

One of the highlights of our school years was attending the Homeschool Book Fair in a nearby city. There were literally thousands of attendees with lots and lots of book vendors, speakers, and interesting workshops for just about any homeschooling need.

One year as I was walking around looking at the curriculum displays, I couldn't help overhearing a mom talking about how much she disliked a certain subject. Her dislike was so intense that her children were aware of her feelings and knew she wanted nothing to do with teaching it. She was happy to find classes that would cover the topic so that she didn't have to teach it to her family. As I heard her talk about her dislike for the subject, my heart immediately heard the Lord speak: "She will miss out on knowing the joy of learning this along with her children."

I thought to myself, *If one of her children has a desire to work in a field of this particular study, she won't be part of the journey.* I made the decision then and there that I would make it a point to enjoy the process of learning what my children were involved with in every season. Whether I liked the subject or not, I didn't want to miss out on cheering them on in an area that didn't personally appeal to me.

There will always be subjects or sports or any number of activities that our children like but we don't. While we don't need to be compelled to partake in every single one, let's purpose to enjoy the process. We can cheer our children on whether we like a certain sport or not, and whether or not we homeschool, we can assist them in their learning of all subjects, even those we don't personally like very much.

Incidentally, throughout our homeschooling, I didn't let on that I didn't like science until my boys were around 10 and 12. I confessed. They laughed. We moved on. The lesson to be learned? You don't have to like something to enjoy it with your children. Unless, of course, it's science.

LET'S PRAY

Father, I'm so thankful for the opportunity to help my children learn about so many things. I'm grateful to teach them and learn alongside them. May I always be aware of their interests so that I can help them learn and grow in those areas. In Jesus' name, Amen.

ACTIVITY

Whether you homeschool your children or they attend a private or public school, make it a habit to ask them regularly what they find interesting. You may be surprised to hear what they want to learn about or what they find difficult to understand. Either way, you'll be better prepared to help them and enjoy studying together.

KEEPING THE SABBATH

Remember to observe the Sabbath day by keeping it holy. You have six days each week for your ordinary work, but the seventh day is a Sabbath day of rest dedicated to the Lord your God. On that day no one in your household may do any work ... For in six days the Lord made the heavens, the earth, the sea, and everything in them; but on the seventh day he rested. That is why the Lord blessed the Sabbath day and set it apart as holy.

Exodus 20:8–11

Here is a beautiful truth about the Sabbath: God made it for you! This day is set aside each week and allows you to focus your attention on your relationship with Him. It also brings renewed strength to your body, soul, and spirit.

When my husband was on tour playing golf, our young sons and I traveled with him the majority of the time. We loved being together and seeing so much of the United States. The boys and I also spent quite a bit of time in our hotel rooms. To make things more "homey," I'd bring along toys, games, and books. Keep in mind this was back when you could bring lots of luggage when flying! We enjoyed our times together, but it was sometimes challenging for me to get any long periods of rest. One of the things Mike did regularly was drop me off at a bookstore while he and the boys went out on their own. I could read, browse magazines, or just sit and be still with some coffee and Jesus. Those days were so refreshing, and they served as a respite for my heart. They were my Sabbath days.

If you're a single mom, it may take some planning to schedule your weekly Sabbath, but prayerfully see what you can do to make it happen. Regardless of your situation, know that the Lord will meet you whenever and wherever you call out to Him. You can always grab some tea or coffee, your Bible, and your journal and sit in the most comfortable place in your home. Enter His presence with prayers of praise and thanksgiving, and enjoy this time with your Father. This is something we can all do on a regular basis.

Remember that these sacred times with the Lord will help you better listen to what He wants to say regarding yourself, your marriage, and your children.

Jesus regularly went away from the crowds to be alone with the Father (see Luke 5:16). He knew the importance of spending time in God's presence, and He set the example for us. God loves you and wants to speak to your heart about the things that matter to you and to Him. Prayerfully seek God's heart for what a Sabbath looks like for you and your family. You will find your uninterrupted time with the Lord is a gift to yourself and your loved ones.

LET'S PRAY

Father, I'm glad that spending one day a week to rest is Your plan for me and my family. It's easy to forget that the Sabbath is for *us*. It's a gift! In a season of little ones, Sabbaths may look different, but I'm thankful that You know my heart and my desire to be obedient in this area. Help me to honor You in this set-apart time. In Jesus' name, Amen.

ACTIVITY

Pray about what day of the week would work for your Sabbath. If you are married, talk about it with your husband too. Depending on schedules, the days may change. Where there are babies and toddlers and littles to care for, Sabbaths may take on a different look for you. When you seek God's heart for your family, He will show you His perfect plan. It may not look like what you envision, but He will help you because He loves you. God will always make a way for you.

YOU ARE NOT ALONE

For the Lord is the one who shaped the mountains,
  stirs up the winds, and reveals his thoughts to mankind.
He turns the light of dawn into darkness
  and treads on the heights of the earth.
  The Lord God of Heaven's Armies is his name!

Amos 4:13

A s moms, we can find lots of things to worry about. What if the baby doesn't nap? What if the baby naps too long? What if the toddler falls down? What if Jr. gets a cold? What if Susie won't stop crying? What if (fill-in-the-blank) happens? You get the picture. There always seems to be something to cause concern for every stage of our children's growth and development. Consequently, it's difficult not to be apprehensive as our littles grow into biggies. (Yes, I made that word up.)

We can worry ourselves all day long if we forget that we have a Father who loves and cares for us and for our children. He has a plan for our family, and He is able and willing to carry it out. We just need to trust Him and know that He is always with us.

Here is Amos 4:13 in my own words:

The Lord shaped the mountains.
Those windy days? He makes them happen.
He reveals his thoughts to us.

He created our days to begin with dawn's light and end in
darkness.
He walks on the mountains of the earth.
His name is the Lord God of Heaven's Armies!

This verse brings me so much peace and confidence in my
Lord. It serves as a reminder of His love and care as well as His
might and strength. It affirms His wisdom, His power, and His
goodness. God creates, fights on our behalf, and includes us in
what He thinks. Above all, He is God!

There's not one thing that can derail my days with my God
on His throne. Even in the midst of sickness, confusion, or loss,
our heavenly Father is always there to help us and give us all we
need to get through any situation. We are His children. We are
the children of the Lord God of Heaven's Armies!

LET'S PRAY

Father, I'm so grateful that I have nothing to fear for myself or
my family. Knowing that You are always there for me makes
every day easier and more enjoyable. May my life be an example
to my children that they can trust You in all things! In Jesus'
name, Amen.

ACTIVITY

Ask each of your children if there's anything that makes them
feel scared or causes them to worry. Write their responses
down and then pray over your child, letting them know that
God loves them and is always with them. You may want to keep
a journal for each child that will serve as a reminder of what
God has done in their lives. This would make a sweet book of
reminders of God's goodness and faithfulness.

WALKING THROUGH FIRE

When you go through deep waters,
*   I will be with you.*
When you go through rivers of difficulty,
*   you will not drown.*
When you walk through the fire of oppression,
*   you will not be burned up;*
*   the flames will not consume you.*

Isaiah 43:2

E veryone has their own story that reveals where their heart intersected with God's heart. My story is about faith, believing in who God is and not solely in what He does.

From beginning to end, the Bible is filled with miraculous true stories of God's faithfulness. There are the stories of Noah surviving the Flood and Moses leading the Israelites out of Egypt into the Promised Land. We read about God's promise fulfilled when He sent Jesus, the Messiah, to save the world. Next to the story of our Savior, my favorite is about Shadrach, Meshach, and Abednego in Daniel 3. These three young men, taken into captivity by Nebuchadnezzar, had so impressed the king with their wisdom that they were given positions of authority.

One day the king set up a golden statue and declared that everyone must bow and worship it; otherwise, they would be thrown into a blazing furnace (v. 6). The young men refused, which infuriated the king, and he repeated his threat. They replied,

> O Nebuchadnezzar, we do not need to defend ourselves before you. If we are thrown into the blazing furnace, the God whom we serve is able to save us. He will rescue us from your power, Your Majesty. But even if he doesn't, we want to make it clear to you, Your Majesty, that we will never serve your gods or worship the gold statue you have set up (vv. 16–18).

Outraged at their response, King Nebuchadnezzar orders his servants to increase the furnace to seven times its normal temperature. Shadrach, Meshach, and Abednego were tied up and thrown inside. The furnace was so hot that the soldiers who threw them in died from the flames. When the king looked inside the furnace, he couldn't believe his eyes. Not only were the three men untied and unharmed, but there was also a fourth man inside who "looks like a god!" (v. 25). The king immediately called the young men to come out of the furnace. Verse 27 says, "The fire had not touched them. Not a hair on their heads was singed, and their clothing was not scorched. They didn't even smell of smoke!" The king couldn't help but praise God.

These three young men refused to allow their circumstances, even the threat of death, to shake their trust in God. They knew that God could miraculously save them, but they also chose to be faithful. The "even if He doesn't" moments define our faith. This doesn't mean we can't feel confused, sad, or even mad. It means we know that God is in control.

I was sad when we miscarried our first baby. I was sad when Jared didn't survive, and I was sad when our Dani died.

I was confused too. I still don't understand why these things happened, but I know that I know that God has a plan. I have learned to trust Him with both my joys and my heartbreaks. He can be trusted even when things don't go as we may like.

LET'S PRAY

Father, I trust You. I know that You love me and that Your ways are good, even when my circumstances are hard. May my heart always stay held in Your hands, and may my eyes remain focused on You. Regardless of what happens in my life, You are my hope and my salvation. In Jesus' name, Amen.

ACTIVITY

Have you walked through fire—those days or seasons that seem never-ending and insurmountable? If you have, write in your journal how the Lord showed Himself faithful during that time. If you are currently struggling, seek His face and allow His peace, love, and strength to sustain you. He is good, and He loves you fiercely.

WHERE'S THE MAP?

When people do not accept divine guidance, they run wild.

Proverbs 29:18

I t's hard to get from one place to another if you don't know where you're going. I'm not good at reading maps. When I have to get to some place that's new to me, I'll have Mike go over the directions, and I'll write them down and study them. Yes, really. Now, I'm okay with following the directions on my phone when they include line by line instructions. I really like those!

If you need to get from here to there, you need a plan. Whether it's for a trip, a new job, or your parenting, you need vision. These beautiful, tiny humans just want to be loved, fed, and taken care of by their parents. "Taken care of," however, has a rather broad definition. Talk to 10 different people, and you're likely to get 10 different answers.

One of the most important things Mike and I learned early on was the importance of having a vision for our parenting. We had questions that needed answers:

- What kind of parents did we want to be?
- How could we parent our children in a way that would draw them close to us and to the Lord?
- What kind of relationship did we want our children to have with each other?

Anything we wish to do well requires planning, time, patience, work, and lots of prayer. Being Mom is no different. Vision is important because it helps determine the decisions we make on a regular basis. How do we get a vision for life, marriage, and parenting? We seek God's heart by reading His Word and praying for wisdom and guidance. When we have God's vision, we can focus more clearly on Him and what He desires for us and our families.

Make a list of all the things you can consider when seeking God's vision for yourself, your marriage, your children, and anything else that comes to mind. Use the list as a starting point and add any additional topics or categories that you find interesting. You may have some vision ideas for yourself as a mom and wife and some thoughts regarding your children. Keep in mind that the best vision ideas will come straight from God's heart. When we have His plan in sight, we can position ourselves to receive the wonderful things He has for us and our families.

Simple Steps for Vision Planning:

- Pray alone, and, if married, pray with your husband.
- Listen to hear what God puts on your hearts.
- Read the Word.
- Write everything that comes to mind.
- Clarify the vision.
- Make a plan.
- Repeat as needed.

Having a vision is great, but it shouldn't replace praying and hearing the Lord every day. Review the lists you made every few months. Continue to pray and welcome God to make any changes and to be in control of your direction. His guidance will always be best.

LET'S PRAY

Father, thank You for Your beautiful vision for my family. My heart's desire is to follow You and know Your plan for every area of our lives. I pray that You will guide me and help me to hear Your voice as you lead us each day. It is in your perfect will that I desire my family to be. In Jesus' name, Amen.

ACTIVITY

Once your family vision is written, discuss it with your children. Let them know that you and their dad have prayed and sought God's heart for His guidance. Together, pray and thank the Lord for His love and protection. Display a copy of your family vision in a place where the whole family can see it.

DAY 46

READY, SET, GO!

Children are a gift from the Lord;
they are a reward from him.
Children born to a young man
are like arrows in a warrior's hands.
How joyful is the man whose quiver is full of them!

Psalm 127:3–5

I love that our children are compared to arrows in this Scripture. Arrows are made to be sent out. They have a purpose, and the same is true of our children. Every child has a God-given purpose, and in His perfect timing, he or she will walk in that special calling. Are you putting into practice now what will enable and empower your children to hit the mark in the future?

When an arrow is released, multiple factors can influence whether or not it will reach its desired target. Some of these factors may include wind, temperature, sunlight, the tension of the bow, and, of course, the archer. As parents, we are the archers holding our children's hearts and preparing them to be released. Countless decisions will be made over the course of their childhood and young adult years, which can affect the direction of their lives. This isn't intended to scare you or make you worry. On the contrary, it should encourage your prayers and planning.

Vision provides direction. Ask yourself, *Where am I aiming my children?* If there is no target, where will they land? One of the benefits of having God's vision for your children is that He will direct your steps. Vision also sets a boundary that helps you make daily, ongoing decisions for yourself and your family.

My husband and I have a small ranch about 90 minutes from our home in town. To get to our property, you have to unlock the gate with a key. If a thief really wanted to, he could drive straight through the gate, but he would likely hurt himself and his vehicle. He could climb over the low gate, but he would have problems getting to our home and carrying away anything he wanted to steal. The point to all this is that while someone could potentially break in, it would be difficult because we have done everything we can to keep our ranch safe from harm. When you know there's the possibility of danger, you do all you can to protect the people you love. Boundaries provide protection. When you have a vision for your family, it will help you provide the boundaries you need.

Make decisions with the end goal in mind. If you want to have a good and loving relationship with your children as they get older, what do you need to do now to ensure that will happen? If you want them to have a strong walk with the Lord, what needs to be put in place to help them with that? Seek God's heart for the vision He has for your children. He has a plan for every family, and each one of your children is part of that plan.

LET'S PRAY

Father, I know Your plans are good for my children. Thank You for giving them the talents and strengths they need to walk in the way that You have designed for them. Give me wisdom as I encourage and help them walk in the vision You have for them. In Jesus' name, Amen.

ACTIVITY

Enjoy all the moments with your children as you watch them grow. Each season will give you more glimpses into their strengths and possible callings. As you pray for your sons and daughters, write down any thoughts or impressions the Lord puts on your heart. These will serve as prayer points for you as your children get older.

ALL THE SIGNS

God is our refuge and strength,
always ready to help in times of trouble.

Psalm 46:1

Last spring, we had a severe thunderstorm in our town that brought lots of rain and hail. This all resulted in severe roof damage to many homes, including ours. Driving around nearby neighborhoods, Mike and I noticed roofing signs in the front yards of numerous homes. The signs served as advertisements for the various roofing businesses, and they let everyone know what companies were contracted to work on any particular home's roof. We even had one of these signs gracing our front yard for several months.

During this time, Mike and I were driving home one day, and as I noticed all the signage, a thought came to mind: *What if each of our homes had a sign that listed our struggles, worries, and concerns? Or what if we had signs that told the world about our walk with the Lord?* Instead of a Roofing Repairs sign, there could be these signs:

- Need God
- Haven't Prayed in Months
- Haven't Read the Bible ... Ever
- Heart Repairs

- Marriage Repairs
- Friendship Repairs
- Relationship with Children Repairs

At one time or another, we have all needed damage repair for our lives. Obviously, we don't need to hang out signs about our personal difficulties, but we don't need to keep them hidden either. Everyday there are many of us facing situations that require some kind of damage control or repair. As women, wives, moms, business owners, and humans, life happens, and it isn't always easy.

Thankfully, instead of calling a repair company, we can call God. Take a moment to steady yourself and cry out to Him. He sees you. He knows what you're going through, and He wants to help. He won't push Himself on you, though. Ask Him. He's there, ready, willing, and able to help you when you ask. No sign required.

There are Christian churches and ministries that can help you find the assistance you need. Call a trusted friend or family member who will help you as you take the first step toward healing. God loves you, and the signs of His love are all around you.

LET'S PRAY

Thank You, Father, for knowing what I need when I can't see clearly. You are always there to help me in every situation that comes my way. Help me remember that You are my Savior, my Redeemer, and my ever-present help in times of trouble. I love You. In Jesus' name, Amen.

ACTIVITY

Make a list of all the times you can remember when God has helped you through a difficult situation or season. The Lord may have provided help through a friend, or perhaps a situation was resolved without any fallout. Whatever the case may be, write it down and keep this ongoing list as a reminder of how much God cares for you.

DO I NEED A NEW PRESCRIPTION?

But you are always the same;
you will live forever.

Psalm 102:27

I've worn glasses off and on since I was two years old. Apparently, I had a lazy eye that prompted my parents to take me to the eye doctor. What followed were constant glasses throughout my elementary school years, sporadic glasses during high school, and pretty much no glasses through college and work that followed. I got married and had children. Then about 15 years ago, I found that while my long-distance eyesight was still good, reading required those glasses again. Today, I wear them regularly. They're somewhat of a fashion accessory as well as a much-needed component to seeing more clearly.

Why the "seeing" history? I have learned that how we "see" something today may not be how we see that same thing tomorrow. For example, decorating ideas come and go. Growing up, my family had avocado green carpet in our living room. Now, I do not see that ever making a comeback. But some of the furniture we had in my childhood home is now considered retro or mid-century. The same is true for clothing. My young school days brought bellbottom pants, platform shoes, and hair parted down the middle. Guess what girls are wearing today?

While there are changes over the years regarding style, décor, and a number of other things, God never changes, and neither does His Word.

The grass withers and the flowers fade,
but the word of our God stands forever (Isaiah 40:8).

We can trust that what the Bible says is true every day, all the time, no matter what. Yes, there will be voices that try to bring new definitions or bend the meaning to suit their own agendas, but God's Word is His Word, and it will not be changed to suit the culture.

This is important for all the moms out there who have children of all ages in all stages. Our children are bombarded with half-truths, which means these are half-lies. The problem is, we can't see the lie if we don't know the truth. Reading the Word for ourselves and to our children will help us all know God's voice. From the time they are littles, reading and talking about God's Word will help them have a firm foundation to discern the truth from all the noise of the world.

My glasses help me see and read God's Word, but it's the Word that helps my mind, heart, soul, and spirit see, hear, and know God. He never changes; He is the same yesterday, today and forever!

LET'S PRAY

Father, give me a hunger to read, know, and love Your Word. May my heart recognize the truths in the Bible when I'm confronted with the lies the world throws at me. I choose to follow You today and always. In Jesus' name, Amen.

ACTIVITY

Keep a journal to write down the Scriptures that speak to your heart while reading the Bible. This will serve as a personal collection of encouragement from God's Word.

SECTION 6

A LASTING LEGACY

So each generation should set its hope anew on God,
not forgetting his glorious miracles
and obeying his commands.

Psalm 78:7

From the time our children come into our world, we are creating a legacy. What will your family legacy be? Rest assured; God has a plan for each of our families. We just need to ask Him.

SO MANY NAMES

A good name is to be chosen rather than great riches,
Loving favor rather than silver and gold.

Proverbs 22:1 (NKJV)

I have always wondered why the Bible contains so many lists of people. The Old Testament—1 and 2 Chronicles in particular—has numerous lists of tribes, clans, and families. There are so many names! One day it struck me that while all these lists of names and families are a good thing historically speaking, they are also important because families are important to God. Families are comprised of people, and people are important to God. These biblical lineages and lists of names are the history of our world, and each of our personal family lines is no less important to our Father. Our ancestral heritage matters to Him, and it should matter to us.

How many times have you heard someone say, "Oh, I can see your great grandmother's eyes in your little one" or "He sings as beautifully as his daddy"? Perhaps Grandma's gorgeous red hair makes its appearance when a baby is born. Maybe it's that quick wit that brings a smile of remembrance to your heart. Whatever the similarity or likeness, there is that "Aha!" moment of recognition that binds the generations.

When I was pregnant with my sons, I prayed they would be strong and athletic like their dad. I really did! You see, I'm not very good at sports. Strike that, I'm not good at all at sports. I like them a lot, but that's where my sports ability starts and ends. Mike, on the other hand, prayed that they'd be happy and joyful like me. I think we both got our prayers answered!

While many couples bring a rich and godly foundation into their families, not everyone will have an endearing or memorable family heritage. Some of us may carry the hurts or misguided decisions from our families or from our own past. Thankfully, Jesus Christ brings redemption. He can redeem any mistake, bad decision, or difficult family history. Our Savior makes all things new!

> This means that anyone who belongs to Christ has become a new person. The old life is gone; a new life has begun! (2 Corinthians 5:17).

When Jesus died and rose again, He made a way for us to begin anew. We are new creations set apart for Him. That, my friend, is the foundation for a new family heritage!

LET'S PRAY

Father, I am so grateful for my children. Thank You that the name of Jesus is the foundation of our home and family. With Your guidance, help me teach my children the beauty of family and the gift of living out a legacy for future generations. In Jesus' name, Amen.

ACTIVITY

Prayerfully ask the Lord to give you a word or Scripture for your family. Write it down, frame it, and place it where it can be seen by everyone in the house.

LIVING A LEGACY

Good people leave an inheritance to their grandchildren,
but the sinner's wealth passes to the godly.

Proverbs 13:22

Whether we plan to or not, we all have a legacy. You may be a single mom, married without children, or married with children. Whatever your circumstances, you will have a legacy. You may wonder, *What if I don't have a history worth sharing?* The truth is, we don't all have wonderful life stories that we want to be passed down to our children. We can, however, still share what God has done to redeem our lives and our futures. We can share how He brought us from a hurting past to a place of redemption, healing, and restoration. If this is your family's story, then this is part of your legacy.

When it comes to family, legacy is defined as "something transmitted by or received from an ancestor or predecessor or from the past."[1] If we see legacy as a passing down of ideals, it becomes a beautiful gift. I encourage you to think about these questions:

- How do you want your family to be remembered?
- What do you want them to be known for in the future?

---

1. *Merriam-Webster.com Dictionary*, s.v. "legacy," accessed December 14, 2021, https://www.merriam-webster.com/dictionary/legacy.

- When your family name is said, what do you want it to stand for?
  - Hospitality?
  - Extravagant giving?
  - Caring for the downtrodden?
- Will your family be known as prayer warriors or the joy-filled tribe?

Your family is a legacy in the making. When you recognize the intangible gifts that were passed down to you, you will more readily realize the importance of stewarding what you have been given. Some of these gifts are lessons learned from past generations so that future loved ones can learn from mistakes made and choose more wisely. Other gifts will be the laying down of a strong foundation, enabling others to build and grow from past successes. When we see the blessings that are passed down to us, it becomes our responsibility to steward them well and to continue adding to the legacy that's been established over the generations. It's about choosing to be deliberate in our actions, in our words, and in our choices.

Mike and I came to know Jesus as our Lord and Savior one year into our marriage. This changed everything we did as a couple and as parents. We made our Christian faith the foundation of our family. God's Word became our guide for life, and the power of the Holy Spirit became our strength. We are not perfect, but we serve a perfect Father.

What is your family legacy? Seek the Father's heart because He has a plan for your loved ones, and it's good!

LET'S PRAY

Father, I am overwhelmed by Your goodness! You care for me and my family with a love that that never ceases. That is a lasting legacy of Your faithfulness. May our love for others be a testimony of who You are, and may our lives bring You glory every day. In Jesus' name, Amen.

ACTIVITY

Prayerfully seek God's heart for your family's legacy. There is no pressure in this exercise, because He will show you as you continue to ask Him. Your family legacy may already be evident to you. Perhaps you are cheerful givers of time or gifts or finances. You may find that praying for others is what defines your family. Whatever it may be, find the joy in it. It is your family legacy that will speak to future generations.

A LEGACY OF FAITH AND FAMILY

Let each generation tell its children of your mighty acts;
let them proclaim your power.

Psalm 145:4

W ithout a doubt, the best thing we can pass down to our children is a living and active love for Jesus. We want them to know that He is the Lord and Savior of our lives. This sounds great, but how do we do this? One moment at a time.

Our everyday lives will offer us endless opportunities to share about God and His love for us. We can talk about how Jesus came into the world so that He could one day die for our sins and then rise again to give us eternal life. This may sound simplistic, but the salvation story is beautifully simple.

- Jesus was born.
- He lived a sinless life. We all make mistakes, but Jesus never did.
- Jesus loves us so much that He died for our sins.
- He rose again so that we could have eternal life one day in heaven.
- When we ask Him to be our Lord and Savior, He will!

For everyone has sinned; we all fall short of God's glorious standard. Yet God, in his grace, freely makes us right in his sight. He did this through Christ Jesus when he freed us from the penalty for our sins (Romans 3:23–24).

When our sons were young, we went through a two-and-a-half-year span in which we suffered the loss of many loved ones. These included Mike's sister, the baby son we miscarried, my mom, Mike's dad, and our baby daughter, Dani, who died from a chromosomal abnormality. It was a difficult season.

Our children, however, were able to see what it means to live a life of faith. We were sad, we cried, and we called out to God for His strength. Our hope was that our young sons would know that in spite of any situation, God is in control. He loves us no matter what, and even when our prayers aren't answered the way we would like, He is a good and loving Father. Ultimately, our faith is not based on what God does but on who He is. That is a legacy of faith.

LET'S PRAY

Father, our faith in You is our shield and protection from any difficulty. No one ever completely knows the hurts of our hearts except You. It is only by Your love and compassion that we are able to live through all this life throws at us. Thank You that Your strength is always more than enough to get us through every tear we may shed. You are faithful! In Jesus' name, Amen.

ACTIVITY

Set aside time each week to write down what the Lord has done to show Himself faithful. It could be something as profound as His miraculous provision for an unforeseen financial burden.

It could be one of the simple yet beautiful joys of seeing His love through the eyes of your little ones. Keeping a journal of these "faith" gifts serves to remind us that we are always on our Father's heart. He loves you!

BUILDING ALTARS

So Joshua called together the twelve men he had chosen—one from each of the tribes of Israel. He told them, "Go into the middle of the Jordan, in front of the Ark of the Lord your God. Each of you must pick up one stone and carry it out on your shoulder— twelve stones in all, one for each of the twelve tribes of Israel. We will use these stones to build a memorial. In the future your children will ask you, 'What do these stones mean?' Then you can tell them, 'They remind us that the Jordan River stopped flowing when the Ark of the Lord's Covenant went across.' These stones will stand as a memorial among the people forever."

Joshua 4:4–7

In the Old Testament, altars were built as offerings to God that would serve as memorials of what He did in people's lives. As His children, have you set any stones in place to serve as reminders of what the Lord has done in your family's life?

During the course of life, we will find places of struggle and possible hardship. If we rely on God, we will see how He gets us through it, either by removing the obstacle or by taking our hand and walking us through it. It's during these times that we can create altars that will serve as memorials to God's hand moving in our situation.

What do modern-day altars look like? They are anything that serves as a reminder of God's faithfulness and love. They are also family traditions that keep the joy of being together special and memorable.

Sharing Stories: Talking about moments where God's hand was evident builds our family's faith. One story we regularly talked about when our boys were little was how our son Joel was healed from what the doctor believed was cancer. It has served as a reminder of God's miraculous healing power.

Celebrating Special Anniversaries: In our family we celebrate the day our baby girl was born in July, and two months and six days later, we commemorate the day she went to heaven.

Family Traditions that Are Unique to Your Family: When our sons were little, we slept under the Christmas tree on Christmas Eve. For Valentine's Day we had a basket filled with goodies for them. Resurrection Day was always a day for celebrating our resurrected Lord with church services, yummy food, and a basket filled with gifts and treats. This basket was one they had to look for as it was hidden somewhere in the house.

Our Family Nighttime Prayer: We prayed Numbers 6:24–26 over our boys every night. The last times we prayed this over them were the nights before their wedding days.

Birthdays: When our boys were young, there were parties, and as they got older it was usually a family dinner with close friends. On their 13th birthdays, Mike took them out for breakfast or lunch and invited several men who were important in their lives to speak words of encouragement over them. We still have the videos of these special birthdays.

Sharing God-stories and celebrating special days with our children will do several things:

- Build their faith in the Lord.
- Build their reliance on God for today and for the future.
- Make God a reality in their lives.

Let me encourage you: your family legacy is *yours*. It will be unique because your family is one of a kind. There is no other family like yours on this planet! Lean into the Lord, and He will show you how to celebrate your loved ones.

LET'S PRAY

Father, I'm so grateful that we have much to be thankful for and to celebrate! Even in the most difficult seasons, we can rejoice in Your love and goodness. Most importantly, we can celebrate knowing Jesus as our Lord and Savior. Help me find ways to celebrate all those things that make our family special. In Jesus' name, Amen.

ACTIVITY

Seek God's heart and write a Celebration List. What events do your family want to celebrate? When the budget is short and the list is long, remember that just being together over dinner can be a party when someone is being celebrated! There's no need for gifts when words of encouragement and love are expressed. Find ways to set up memorials for your family. They will serve as beautiful memories.

WRITE IT DOWN

Beautiful words stir my heart.
I will recite a lovely poem about the king,
for my tongue is like the pen of a skillful poet.

Psalm 45:1

I've never been consistent with journaling. I love journals, and I have quite a few of them, but I haven't always written in them. A few years ago my friend Arling gave me a beautiful journal with Scriptures and godly quotes written on every page. I decided to make it my prayer journal. While I didn't use it every day, I made it a point to write in it regularly. I wrote what was on my heart. I wrote prayer requests and any dreams I had and what they might mean.

That year turned out to be a time of quite a few situations that required a lot of prayer. I wrote everything down in my journal—the cries of my heart, the pain of walking through this tough season, and the daily prayer needs of a woman, wife, and mom needing wisdom, courage, and strength. Like I said, everything.

Today, years later, it is amazing to go back and see all God has done in my life and in the lives of my family. I am not exaggerating when I say that the Lord has done miracles!

I encourage you to keep a journal. Make it easy by writing simple phrases of what's happening in your world. Jot down your prayer requests and anything that is heavy on your heart. Write your prayers. You don't have to write every single thing, but write those things that are important to you. Again, it doesn't have to be overly detailed.

Then write down what God does in answer to your prayers. Here's the thing: the answers may not be what you thought they'd be, or it may take a while before they are answered. The important thing is to seek God's heart and trust in His timing and His answers. He loves you, and He can always be trusted even when we don't understand.

Journaling your prayers will serve as a reminder of God's answers and as an altar of what God has done in your life and in the lives of your family. It'll serve as a reminder of who He is, and it'll be an encouragement as you continue to seek Him.

Write it down so that you won't forget. Life tends to get in the way of a good memory. We forget even the most important things and days in our lives. Not only do we sometimes forget what the Lord has already done, but we also forget what He can do, what He does do, and what He will do. So write it down!

LET'S PRAY

Father, thank You that You always answer when I cry out to You. It may not always look the way I thought it would or come in my preferred timing. But I know You can always be trusted. Your answers and your timing are always going to be best. I love You, and I trust You completely. Thank You, Lord! In Jesus' name, Amen.

ACTIVITY

If journaling is new to you, try writing just two or three days a week. Be sure to write down any answers to your prayer requests. You can also journal any thoughts or questions that come up during your daily Bible reading. Just remember to write it down!

DAY 54

LITTLE BY LITTLE

I will teach all your children,
and they will enjoy great peace.

Isaiah 54:13

I f your children are past the age of littles, you will probably find yourself saying something like, "They grow up so fast. One minute they're little, and the next they're grown." It's true. While the days of changing diapers and all-nighters can seem endless, they really are relatively short. The adult years will surpass the younger years. Every season has its incredible joys when you are purposeful to make them happen. Our littles will grow up, and little by little we will release them.

It starts with holding our babies' hearts and little bodies. We hold them close in our efforts to keep them safe and secure.

As they begin learning to walk, we hold on to each little hand, helping them stay steady on their little feet. Sometimes they fall, but they learn to get up. Our hands are always there, just inches away to help them.

As our children grow, we help them cross the street and stay safely with us in crowded places by holding their hand and their heart.

As they get a bit older and begin to navigate different areas of life, we keep a hand at the ready for a pat on the back or a needed hug, all the while still holding their hearts.

Then there's the years of adolescence. Let me encourage you: while there can be challenges as our children learn to make decisions for themselves, they still need our attention and input and pats on the back and hugs, sometimes more than ever. While we may not have been holding their hands for a while, we do continue to hold their hearts.

Before you know it, your children are adults. By this time, you've hopefully and prayerfully come to a place of having a loving relationship as friends, as well as still being Mom. They honor you, not only because God's Word calls them to do so, but also because you've created a healthy atmosphere of mutual love and respect over the years. Their hearts are no longer yours to hold, because they are grown. But even if they are married and have children of their own, you are still connected by love.

Mike and I had one primary goal for our children: to know Jesus as their Lord and Savior. And while I always told them I was their cheerleader when they were young, I also let them know that one day they would fall in love and get married. Their wives would become their best friends and number one cheerleaders! You see, we are in a journey of releasing our children little by little, in every season and in every passing year. Instead of looking at this as a sad thing, rejoice in knowing that you are creating beautiful memories and moments that will lay the foundation for their future families. It's a foundation they can build on for their children and grandchildren, little by little.

LET'S PRAY

Father, the season of having young children can be tiring and sometimes overwhelming. Help me see past the weariness so that I can truly enjoy these moments. Give me ideas that will help me make these growing years memorable and fun for all of us! Thank You for my family. They are a blessing. In Jesus' name, Amen.

ACTIVITY

When ideas come to mind regarding activities, parties, or field trips, write them down as soon as you can. It's easy to forget things when our hands are literally and figuratively full. Even as a grandmom, if I don't write it down, it isn't gonna happen! Keep a running list in your journal or notebook. You'll be glad you did.

LETTING GO

When I was a child, I spoke and thought and reasoned as a child.
But when I grew up, I put away childish things.

1 Corinthians 13:11

From the time our children are born, we are in a constant state of letting go. As babies, our children rely on us 100 percent to feed, nurture, and love them. As our children grow, they naturally become less and less dependent on us. They learn to feed and dress themselves, and before we know it, they are driving and studying for a career.

As your children mature, you will find that they need you less and less. While that may seem weird and almost sad, it's really a good thing. Their dependence on you must diminish as their dependance on God grows. This doesn't mean you won't have a close relationship. On the contrary, even with adult children, you can still be close and available to them should they ever need your input.

While we have the upper hand in "discussions" with our young ones, once they are older, all bets are off. Young adults will have thoughts, feelings, opinions, and ideas all their own. And isn't that what we want? Don't we want to raise our children to speak up and share their thoughts, ideas, and opinions? Of course we do. We want our sons and daughters to have the confidence to speak their minds with a healthy dose of honor and respect.

"But what if we don't agree?" you might ask. Buckle up! You won't always agree. As our children become adults, they will have their own outlook on things. I'm not talking about anything unbiblical that goes against God's Word. It's all the other things of life that our children may see differently than their parents.

Here's what I've come to understand as my sons have grown, matured, married, and become fathers: we aren't always going to agree on everything, but as long as we love and respect each other, we'll always land on love. Always.

Landing on love is the goal for our relationship with our adult children. My prayer and hope are that they will grow in their walks with the Lord and in their love with their wives and that they will follow God's Word for their marriages and lives.

Our sons and daughters are under our care for a short time. They do not belong to us; they belong to the Father. We are not one with our children, nor are we called to be. We are called to be one with our spouse. The beauty of a Christian family, though, is that we are all one with the Father. Loving and serving Him is the greatest common denominator in any family relationship.

LET'S PRAY

Father, thank You for my family. I'm grateful we can talk and share and even disagree sometimes. I'm glad we can share our thoughts and still honor each other. Help me walk in wisdom and understanding. May we all continue to grow in You and in our love for You and our families. In Jesus' name, Amen.

ACTIVITY

What does "landing on love" look like in regard to your adult children? If you're not sure, ask the Lord to show you. He will give you ideas that will work specifically for your family.

LOVE ALWAYS

Be on guard. Stand firm in the faith. Be courageous. Be strong. And do everything with love.

1 Corinthians 16:13–14

We're called to be "on guard," which means to be awake and vigilant. It's a military description for a sentinel who keeps watch to ensure safety from enemy attack. We're told to stand firm, be courageous, be strong, and do all this in love. That's the key, isn't it? That all we do and say be done in love. That's why God sent Jesus to be our Savior. Because He loves us. That's why Jesus died on the cross for us and rose again. Because He loves us. He loves us!

But anyone who does not love does not know God, because God is love (1 John 4:8).

How do we do "everything" with love? We pray. We seek God's heart for strength and wisdom. And we speak words that convey our love as much as possible. Here are some important words and phrases we can use regardless of our children's ages:

- God loves you.
- I love you.
- I love you more.
- I forgive you.

- I'm sorry.
- Please forgive me.
- Thank you!
- You're welcome.
- Way to go!
- I'm proud of you!

"I love you more." I cannot tell you how many times I said that to my sons when they were young. They would reply, "I love you more." After going back and forth a couple of times, I would cheerfully tell them, "No, I love you more because I'm your mother." That says it all. We love more because we're moms.

Make it a daily goal to find the joy of being Mom. It's in the everyday moments that make up motherhood where the lifelong memories are made. From the moment we hold our newborns, to the wet kisses from our toddlers, to the hugs from children who grow taller than we are, to the moment we look into their eyes on their wedding days ... find the joy of being Mom.

If you're in the trenches and finding it hard to have joy, hang in there. Joy is right around the corner of sleepless nights, brain fog, and seemingly endless crying (yours and the baby's). Reach out to the One who created you and yours. God is on call 24/7. He loves you. He sees you. His plans for you, your marriage, and your children are so good!

> May our sons flourish in their youth
>   like well-nurtured plants.
> May our daughters be like graceful pillars,
>   carved to beautify a palace.
> May our barns be filled
>   with crops of every kind.

May the flocks in our fields multiply by the thousands,
  even tens of thousands,
  and may our oxen be loaded down with produce.
May there be no enemy breaking through our walls,
  no going into captivity,
  no cried of alarm in our town squares.
Yes, joyful are those who live like this!
  Joyful indeed are those whose God is the Lord
  (Psalm 144:12–15).

LET'S PRAY

Father, You are my steady rock. It is because of Your wisdom and help that I can find joy in being Mom. I'm so grateful! Thank You for my children. Each one is a treasure. My cup is filled to overflowing with Your goodness and love. Thank You! In Jesus' name, Amen.

ACTIVITY

Read 1 Corinthians 13:4–7. Go verse by verse and study them. You'll be so encouraged by what the Lord is telling you in these Scriptures.

DAY 57

SLEEPLESS NIGHTS

Children are a gift from the Lord;
they are a reward from Him.

Psalm 127:3

Our son Joel and his wife, Danny, recently had a beautiful baby girl. Melody is sweet, with big brown eyes and dark brown hair. She is a doll!

When our daughter-in-love was pregnant, Mike and I made it a point to encourage her and Joel on being parents. We shared how wonderful it would be to hold their little one and watch her grow. We shared sweet stories of when Joel and his brother were little. So fun!

What we didn't mention was that we hardly slept that first week or two. We had to adjust to a baby's needs, and we had to really give of ourselves like never before. We weren't trying to hide anything from them. On the contrary, we shared what stood out most in our minds, which was the joy we had in being Mom and Dad!

Just days into their newfound journey as parents, Joel and Danny shared that all was getting better after a few sleepless nights ... and days. It was then that we shared our stories of tiredness and fear of not knowing if we were doing everything right. We shared how we had struggled with wondering if were being "good" parents. We told them that we never intentionally kept our early parenting days from them; we simply didn't think about it.

You see, once you get past the first few days (or weeks), things really do get better. You and the baby will start sleeping better. He or she will start nursing better, or if you use bottles, you will get into a routine that works for everyone. Allow me to add that it can sometimes take even longer than a few weeks for things to settle down for you as you walk this new path of mothering. Every baby is different. The Bible tells us in 2 Corinthians 10:12 that comparing ourselves with others is not smart. Every parent must prayerfully do what's best for their family.

For one baby it might be sleepless nights, but for me it was sleepless days. Joel never did take great daily naps. On occasion he would sleep, but that was the exception. I didn't complain, though, because he regularly slept through the night at two weeks old. It had nothing to do with anything I did. It was just him.

All this to say, every baby is different. Some will sleep more than others. In the long scheme of things, it's a short season. I promise that when they get older, you'll have time to nap! Enjoy the moments now.

LET'S PRAY

Father, please help me to be fully present at every moment with my littles. Even when sleep is a distant memory, keep me focused on the blessing of my children. I trust You to give me the strength and energy I need for each day. In Jesus' name, Amen.

ACTIVITY

Are you in a season of little sleep? Rest when you can and allow a trusted friend to help you if possible. You can take a needed nap while she watches the baby. Write down a few verses that will help keep you focused on God's love and faithfulness. Keep them in places where you will see them throughout the day.

THE JOY OF BEING (GRAND)MOM

Grandchildren are the crowning glory of the aged;
parents are the pride of their children.

Proverbs 17:6

My given name is Judith, but everyone knows me as Judy. My husband usually calls me Honey or Babe. My children call me Mom. To my grandchildren, I am Mia (my grandmom name). I'm Hispanic and thought it would be nice to have a name that is easy to say in English and in Spanish. I also love that in Spanish, Mia means 'mine.'

Over the years, virtually every woman I know who is a grandmom has said that it's the best thing ever! Even better than being Mom. I would hear them say this and wonder, *How can it be better than being Mom to your own children?* Even after I became Mia, I wondered how it could possibly be better than motherhood.

Well, with almost a year of being Mia under my belt, I think I understand. Parenting our own children brings with it many responsibilities. There's discipline, which involves teaching, training, and correction. There are the ongoing decisions regarding the care of the children, not to mention the daily "to dos" and "have tos" that come with being Mom.

When it comes to being a grandmom, however, there really aren't that many decisions to make. That's because the majority of the decisions are already made for us by their parents. We just do what we're told and follow the instructions we are given. What freedom! We can simply enjoy our time together and have fun without wondering what to do. We know what Mom and Dad want, and we just carry it out. What a relief not to have to think it through or wonder how to handle things!

Our biggest decisions are along the lines of what game to play and how many times to play the same game; when to take a walk; how many cookies should I give him/her (unless we've already been told); and can I just take a nap with them?!

In all seriousness, I absolutely loved being Mom. The joys of seeing my sons take their first steps and speak their first words are some of the things I will forever treasure. And those sweet hugs and kisses are beautiful memories that live in my heart. Today, I get to make new memories with the grands, and while I may not carry the daily responsibilities of parenting, I am responsible to honor what my children ask of me and their dad. I value our relationship and am happy to carry out whatever instructions I'm given. It's a wonderful season, and I am overwhelmed with such joy. I get it now. Being Mia is awesome! What a blessing!

LET'S PRAY

Father, I'm a grandmom, and my cup is overflowing with thanksgiving at Your faithfulness. Thank you for each of my blessings! I pray Your blessing and favor over each of my grands. May they come to know You as their Lord and Savior at an early age, and may they love and serve You all the days of their lives. In Jesus' name, Amen.

ACTIVITY

One thing I've learned in the short time that I've been Mia is that I don't really need lots of things to keep the littles entertained. Playing with a few dishes and musical toys makes them happy. Having a few books to read is always a good idea, and keeping a stroller at our home makes daily strolls a fun excursion.

IT'S ALL ABOUT RESPECT

Be devoted to one another in love. Honor one another above yourselves.

Romans 12:10 (NIV)

As I write this, I've been Mia for almost a year. While I know I still have a lot to learn, I do believe that I have recognized something that is very important in the relationships we have with our adult children who have children of their own. Simply put, it's respect. We want to respect their concerns, their decisions, and how they choose to parent their children—the key word being *their* children. As a grandparent, my primary responsibility is to honor whatever they ask of me as a grandmom. This includes but is not limited to: when the baby goes to sleep, how the baby goes to sleep, how the baby is cared for, and what and when the baby does or needs anything at all. In other words, the parenting is up to them.

Being Mia is a blessing, and I get to have fun and joy in following the plan my sons and their wives have in place. As for my plan? Well, that's easy. My plan is to continue this way of grandparenting as the grands get older. Easy peasy!

Mike and I have made it clear to our children that we respect and honor their positions as Mom and Dad. Our opinions are just that—our opinions. They are kept to ourselves unless asked for. If we have an idea or thought about something, we ask if we can speak into a situation. Hopefully, our kids have come to realize that we are in their corner. We are grandparents who love them and are for them. That will never change!

Don't misunderstand, though. We don't always do the grand-parenting things perfectly. Mike and I are sometimes lovingly corrected, and we gladly receive that correction because these precious littles are known best by their parents. Our blessing is being able to love them, bless them, and cheer them on—both the grands and our own sons and daughters.

The bottom line is to be respectful, be available, be teachable, and ultimately and most importantly, be a blessing. Interestingly, these are all the things that make any relation-ship strong, kind, and loving!

LET'S PRAY

Father, my heart is overwhelmed with gladness in this new season of being a grandmom. Help me to be a godly example to both my adult children and grandchildren in all that I say and do. May my love, service, and help reflect Your heart for us, Your children. And may I always seek to reflect Your love to those I care about so dearly. With a thankful heart, I pray this in Jesus' name, Amen.

ACTIVITY

Scheduling regular fun activities with the grands is a wonderful way to make sweet memories with them. Consider scheduling one-on-one times with your daughter or daughter-in-love as well. It's important to keep that connection strong and to make time for your own grown-up adventures!

AIR KISSES

"For I know the plans I have for you," says the Lord. "They are plans for good and not for disaster, to give you a future and a hope."

Jeremiah 29:11

Because my grandsons live out of state, I don't get to see them as much as my heart would like. Still, we stay connected through FaceTime and the many wonderful pics that are regularly texted to us by their parents!

During a recent visit, as I held my older grandson, I kissed my finger and told him, "Bennett, these are air kisses. I kiss my finger and wave it around, and the kisses go through the air and find you."

I proceeded to do this for a bit. Each air kiss landed on his cheek, his nose, his chin, his forehead, etc. My thought was that when he's back home, hundreds of miles away from Mike and me, I can throw him air kisses when we FaceTime. Eventually, he'll understand that it's one of our special ways to stay connected.

One morning as Bennett sat on my lap and I was sending air kisses, I was reminded that our heavenly Father sends us, His children, air kisses all the time. These come in many different ways. Perhaps we may be reading our Bible, and a Scripture speaks to our heart and brings tears to our eyes. Air kisses! You may be feeling rushed with an endless to-do list when a calmness suddenly comes over you, and you have the realization that everything is going to be alright. Air kisses! Then there's those dreaded sleepless nights. I remember those. You're tired and have seen the sunrise, and the little one has finally gotten to sleep, but your day is just beginning again. As you prepare for the day, you see your sleeping baby. Beautiful. A gift from God. Your heart swells, and all is well once again. Air kisses!

I believe our days (and nights) are filled with air kisses from our heavenly Father. He loves us so much, and His heart is for us and with us. With every joy-filled moment and every kind gesture, know that the Lord is constantly smiling upon you and sending you His blessings, love, and favor. Or as I like to call them, air kisses.

LET'S PRAY

Father, I'm amazed at the enormity of Your love for me and my family. When my days are full and my nights are long, help me to keep my focus on You. Help me to recognize all the air kisses that You send me every day. I'm so grateful! In Jesus' name, Amen.

ACTIVITY

Make a list of the air kisses you encounter each day. They will serve as a reminder of God's love and faithfulness. Share your list with your older children. They may want to make their own lists as well!

ABOUT THE AUTHOR

J udy and her husband, Mike, have been married more than 32 years. They attend Gateway Church in Southlake, Texas, where Mike is the Executive Pastor to the Senior Pastor. For more than a decade, Judy has enjoyed teaching and speaking on marriage, parenting, and all things Jesus! She has a bachelor's degree in Mass Communications from Pan American University (known today as The University of Texas Rio Grande Valley). Judy and Mike have two adult sons and two wonderful daughters-in-love. Jacob is married to Neeli, and they have two sons—Bennett and Everett. Joel is married to Danielle (Danny), and they have a daughter named Melody.

BUY THE BOOK

Judy Brisky wants you to know that even in the toughest of seasons, you can experience the joy of being a mom every single day. But first you will need help and wisdom that can only come from the Lord. Then you will find that being a mom is one of the most joyful experiences you will ever have. Judy offers the encouragement you need to face common challenges and offers practical solutions from the Bible.

www.gatewaypublishing.com   ISBN: 978-1-951227-47-0